THE HEADACHES
OF
HUMANITY

Ideas That Shape Our Lives

M.B. Walsh

Copyright© 2022
All Rights Reserved
M.B. Walsh

For my great-grandchildren
The wonderful
Teddy & Tallulah
The future belongs to them

TABLE OF CONTENTS

PART ONE:
The Human Condition | 1

1: Life As It Is. 3

PART TWO:
Gimme That Old Time Religion | 7

2: Buddhism: The Rejection 9
3: Judaism:The Perennial Scapegoat 11
4: Christianity: Death and Salvation. 14
5: Islam: Fanaticism and Submission 16
6: Is An Afterlife Possible? 26
7: Is Evil Really So Bad?. 34

PART THREE:
Yang and Yin: The Clash of Opposites | 43

8: Us Versus Them 45
9: Opposing Ideologies. 50
10: Communism. 53
11: Modernism. 57
12: The Romantics. 60
13: Postmodernism: The Counter-Enlightenment 63
14: The Four Horsemen of Postmodernism . . 68

PART FOUR:
To Be or Not To Be | 73

15: To Be 75
16: Not To Be 79
17: The Role of Ritual.. 86

PART FIVE:
The Uncertainty of Certainty | 89

18: The Ordeal of Change 91
19: The Game of Chance 95
20: Disorder and Decay: Things Fall Apart . 101
21: Counter-Entropy: The Biosphere 105

PART SIX:
Laughter & Tears | 109

22: Laughter: The Accessory Reflex 111
23: Humiliation 117
24: Tears: The Tragic View of Life 121
25: Disgust. 126
26: Tragi-Comedy: Celebrities: What Are They For? 131

PART SEVEN:
Art: The Good, the Bad and the Bogus | 137

27: What is Art?. 139
28: What is Beauty? 145
29: The Naked and the Nude. 148

30: Ugliness: A Strangeness in the Proportion ... 151
31: Scatology ... 155
32: The Sublime ... 157

PART EIGHT:
Power | 159

33: The Desire for Power ... 161
34: Leaders and Followers ... 165
35: The Power of Opinion ... 169
36: Naked Power ... 174
37: Revolutionary Power ... 176
38: Economic Power ... 180

PART NINE:
Uncle Scrooge | 187

39: The Secret Life of Money ... 189
40: Is Global Capitalism a Giant Ponzi scheme? ... 196
41: The Banking Casino and its Crooked Croupiers ... 203
42: America is Drowning Not Waving ... 208
43: Boots and Saddles: The American Military Machine ... 216
44: The Washington Snake Pit ... 223

PART TEN:
Fear and Loathing | 229

45: The Greening of Self-Pity City 231
46: The Twilight of the Idols 238
47: All the Heroes Have Left the Building . . 245
48: The Gender Wars 252
49: The Deplorable Whiteness of Being 260
50: Why Are the Oppressed Always So Virtuous? 268
51: The Wonderful World of Work 278
52: How Much Freedom is Enough? 287
53: Are the Old Really Human? 295
About The Author 305

PART ONE

THE HUMAN CONDITION

1

LIFE AS IT IS

BABIES FALL INTO the world like raindrops into a mud puddle. No reason is given. We land as chance will have it, in a good home, or a bad one. In a mud hut or a mansion. Boy or girl. Black, white, or brown. We have no choice in the matter. We are born in blood and pain, between piss and shit. We emerge into the light, completely helpless, without a thought in our empty heads. Our first insult from the world is a slap on the ass to get us breathing. Our first act is a wail of anguish. We are placed in the care of strangers, utterly at the mercy of two giants, our parents, loving or not, who will shape our minds in strange and unpredictable ways.

The lucky child who falls into the arms of a doting mother lives in a kind of paradise where every whim is satisfied, where every tear is tenderly wiped away, where all needs are met and every wish comes true. The unquestioning child takes all this for granted. It seems as if the world and everything in it has been created solely for his benefit. It comes as a numbing shock when the little darling is forced out of the mystic temple of childhood into the cold light of reality. The discovery that the world is a hostile place completely indifferent to our happiness is a body blow from which some never entirely recover.

When we are growing up we begin to notice how unfair the world is. One of the first things we see is inequality. Some people are smarter than others. Some are stronger, faster, better at sports. Others are better-looking, more eloquent, musical or artistic. All these endowments seem to be scattered randomly without rhyme or reason, often to people who least deserve them. None of this seems to be quite fair. So envy and a sense of grievance are planted early on in our hearts.

The world wears a snarling face. Storms, earthquakes, floods, fires and epidemics testify to that. Not to mention the tiger, the wolf, the slithering snake, the mosquito and the tsetse fly. Mother Nature arms her predators with an ingenious array of claws, fangs, suckers, stingers and poisons. To live we must kill either animals or plants. Nature is no believer in disarmament. Life is war.

It's almost as if Mother Earth resents our presence and is doing her best to make existence difficult.

Society, itself, seems to be constructed to make us unhappy. It is made up of rules and regulations, backed up by laws and prisons. It makes demands of us. Society severely limits our individual freedom. It presents us with a host of taboos that thwart and frustrate our desires. Some societies allow greater freedom than others. In North Korea there is no freedom at all. And without freedom, when every day is a struggle for survival, it is impossible to imagine happiness.

Suffering comes from three directions. From our own bodies, from external forces in the world and from other people. Suffering is the default position of human existence. You may be able to avoid taxes, but there is no escape from suffering and death. How we respond to these evils makes us the people that we are.

The young Buddha was a pampered child. He spent his early years in the lap of luxury. He knew nothing of the world beyond the palace walls. Then one day curiosity got the better of him and he decided to venture outside to see what was what. The sight that greeted his eyes knocked him sideways. What he saw was suffering and poverty, hunger and misery. "Why do they live that way?" he asked his tutor.

"Because they have no choice," the tutor replied. "Fate has decreed it so."

A little further on the Buddha was distressed to see a sick man covered in sores. "What's wrong with him?"

"He is full of disease," the tutor replied. "The flesh is prone to all sorts of disgusting afflictions. Fate has decreed it so."

The Buddha's distress increased when he saw a wrinkled, white-haired old man hobbling along supported by a stick. "Why is he so feeble?"

"Because he is old," the tutor replied. "If one lives long enough, the body starts to fall apart. Nothing can prevent it. Fate has decreed it so."

Finally, the Buddha came across a dead man. "Why does he lay so still with blank eyes staring at the sun?"

"Because he is dead," the tutor replied. "Life has left his body, which will soon begin to rot. Everyone must die, even you, little master. Fate has decreed it so."

The Buddha was horrified by these terrible revelations. He rushed back to the palace and shut himself up in a dark room with a cool cloth on his fevered brow. Then he began to think, to wriggle and reason a way out of this existential dilemma. Religions are born out of suffering and the certainty of death.

PART TWO

GIMME THAT OLD TIME RELIGION

2

BUDDHISM: THE REJECTION

WHAT THE BUDDHA eventually came up with was Buddhism, a gospel of renunciation, a life-hating religion that preached complete withdrawal from the world's traffic, renounced all desire, including that of love. Passivity is the key note here. "You must kiss the hand you cannot bite," goes the Oriental proverb. Desire nothing. Enjoy nothing. Love nothing is the Buddhist mantra. A completely empty life is the way to inner calmness and harmony.

In Buddhism there is no heaven, or paradise, nothing to hope for when we die. Only release from the eternal wheel of life. In other words oblivion and death. A glorious state they call Nirvana. Like Christianity it is a religion of punishment. Instead of hell they have reincarnation, the quality of each succeeding life depending on the merits of the last. If we live a bad, unworthy life, then we are condemned to be reborn as something less than human, a dog, or a snail. It's like Snakes and Ladders. One wrong move and you have to start all over again. Buddhism doesn't directly concern itself with human happiness, only with release from existence itself.

The Buddha saw clearly the cause of so much human unhappiness. The cause was Desire. The desire for money, possessions, status, fame, power and all the other wants people yearn for. The Buddha knew such things could not bestow happiness, only a brief cessation from the cattle-prod of Desire. If Desire could be stamped out what a burden would be lifted from the shoulders of humanity, what an impediment to spiritual bliss could be removed.

3

JUDAISM:
THE PERENNIAL SCAPEGOAT

JUDAISM IS A religion of duty. It pioneered monotheism, the belief in one god, not the multitude worshipped by the pagans and the Egyptians. Judaism requires absolute obedience to the laws of this one living God. It offers few rewards. There is no heaven. Not even an afterlife. The Jews accept death, and comfort themselves with the notion that the death of the individual is a small thing compared to the state of felicity and justice ultimately to be achieved by mankind in this world. It offers little solace to the problem of suffering and makes no comment on human happiness. What Judaism does offer is a spiritual home, a sense of belonging to a unified community, a virtuous way of life and the certainty of just laws handed down by God to live by.

The Jews have been great religious thinkers. They were the first to make a clear-cut separation between man and nature. Throughout the ancient world there was a profound sense that the natural world and the human world were intimately connected. This was the very basis for the belief in magic. It was the Jews who debunked cosmic phenomena as the arbiter of man's fate. The Hebrews gave us history rather than superstition.

But that's not all they gave us. They were the first to demonstrate that man can defy the iron law of the survival of the fittest. They turned weakness into strength. They invented fanaticism, the distant hope, and boundless dedication to a faith. With these three weapons of the weak they went out into the world and not only survived, but often confounded the mighty.

Historically, the Jews have been perhaps the most despised and persecuted people on the planet. They had no homeland until after the holocaust when the conscience of the world allowed them a nation of their own called Israel. Before that they wandered the earth, eternal migrants, always unwelcome, always outsiders, always excluded. Nor did they try to assimilate or convert non-Jews. Judaism is not a missionary religion. They resolutely kept themselves separate and vulnerable. The Jews realized that to assimilate with the native population would spell the end of Judaism. A minority that preserves its identity inevitably forms a compact whole which shelters and protects the individual and immunizes him from frustration. For the Jews, suffering and death were far better than losing their identity as a people. When something went wrong in the host society, the Jews were convenient scapegoats. They had no power, no influence, no sympathy and no protection. And yet they managed to survive down the centuries as a widely-scattered community unified by their laws and beliefs. In the case of the Jews suffering and persecution were a positive blessing, a price worth paying.

4

CHRISTIANITY: DEATH AND SALVATION

CHRISTIANITY IS A Jewish heresy. Christ never intended to found a new religion. His mission was to reform Judaism. St Paul was the true founder of Christianity. He did the leg work. He preached the Gospels and spread the word of Christ. Christianity caught on for two main reasons. It relaxed the strict dietary laws of the Jews and allowed the consumption of pork and other forbidden foodstuffs. There is no doubt that the lure of a bacon sandwich drew many eager converts. More importantly it offered something new, an afterlife in a heaven of eternal bliss. To the underclass and the slaves of the Roman Empire – whose lives were nothing but suffering and misery – this was an irresistible message of hope and salvation.

The Christians took the idea of one god from the Jews and the invention of an afterlife from the Egyptians, but complicated and confused things with something called the Trinity. It split God like a piece of wood into three parts: the Father, the Son and the Holy Ghost. This triparty arrangement caused the church a great deal of inner turmoil. It opened the door to controversy and disagreements. It sparked heresies, schisms and theological disputes that often erupted into riot and bloodshed.

Eventually, Christianity became the state religion and grew into a huge monolith that dominated western civilization for a thousand years. Outwardly, it bore a deliberately close resemblance to Plato's Republic. But Plato's Republic contained a fatal flaw the Christians overlooked. It was static, unchanging. Real life doesn't work that way. Life is always changing. It is never still, or entirely stable. Unlike Plato's imaginary Utopia, Christianity grew decadent, lazy and corrupt. The German, Martin Luther, an unhappy, dissatisfied priest, nailed his complaints to a cathedral door and kicked off the Reformation, which gave us Capitalism and all the benefits and all the evils it spawns. The American dream was born in medieval Germany.

5
ISLAM: FANATICISM AND SUBMISSION

ISLAM IS A Christian heresy. It is an aggressive, proselytising religion. It has no scruple in using force to compel unbelievers to fall into line with its ideology. Islam, too, is a one-God system demanding absolute obedience. It didn't make the Christian mistake of cutting God up into slices. So it never experienced the same internal disturbance, except for the power struggle after the prophet's death. Islam is a religion of generous rewards. It offers an afterlife of sensual pleasures in a fragrant garden called Paradise. This Islamic Paradise is a much earthier place than the pale, ethereal heaven of the Christians. It rocks like a waterfront brothel on Saturday night. A great emphasis is put on post mortem sex, a sure way to attract converts.

Obedience is everything. The word 'Muslim' actually means submissive. The ideal believer is a slave. Islam is not a sacerdotal religion. It does not believe in any mediation between God and man. Allah is deaf to petitionary prayers begging for solace or for help. Religion for the Muslim centres on revelation, the word of Allah spoken through his prophets. Allah is also an arbitrary and unpredictable God rather like nature itself. Allah can be cruel and deceptive. He can guide you to paradise, or he can lead you into evil ways along the road to Hell. Whatever he chooses to do his reasons are beyond understanding and question.

A Muslim is required to pray five times a day. This is to insure that God is never far from his thoughts. The devotional exercises of Islam are performed with ease and precision. There are five compulsory practices, or pillars of Islam as they are called.

1. Kalima, or the recital of the creed.
2. Salat, the recital of the five daily prayers, with ablutions.
3. Fasting, especially during the lunar month of Ramadan.

4. Zakat, or almsgiving.
5. Hajj, or pilgrimage to Mecca.

Many would insist that a sixth pillar be added. Jihad, or Holy War.

Islam forbids usury, gambling, pork and alcohol. But there is no prohibition on sex. Polygamy is granted to all.

The pillars of Islam have been planted with innate psychological skill. Nothing is more nicely calculated to create in the worshipper the habitual submission Islam demands. When the drums of Jihad begin to beat, martyrs aren't hard to find. What is a miserable life on earth compared to a fragrant garden where seventy willing virgins are waiting in a private seraglio on the other side of death?

All of these religions offer a formula for living. Christianity and Islam even promise eternal happiness. Buddhism offers release. It seeks escape from the world. Christianity rejects the world. Islam seeks to transform the world. It is ironic that only Judaism, which offers almost nothing, is the single religion out of the big four that affirms the world.

We don't need a tutor to tell us that life is a painful and uncertain affair destined to end in our extinction. Our common experience gives us ample proof of that. It's difficult to decide if the gift of self-awareness, our ability to reason, to understand the cruel situation in which we find ourselves is a blessing or a curse. For what purpose did Nature endow a puny ape with the ability to think? What did she accomplish? This strange new being was smart enough to invent weapons of mass destruction, and stupid enough to turn his world into a stinking slum choking on its own waste. Bestowing apes with intelligence was, without doubt, Nature's greatest blunder. She created a troubled creature with a sick heart and a distressed mind. The other animals have been spared this dubious gift. They have no metaphysics. They are innocent of good and evil. They have no idea that such a thing as death lies in wait. Their lives are untroubled by morbid intellectual speculations. Mother Nature has been kinder to our furry friends than she has been to us.

The awareness of our own certain death is only the beginning of our woes. We are forced to stand helplessly by and watch those we love suffer and die in their turn. The grandparents, the loving mother, the revered father, the brother, the sister, our wives our husbands, perhaps even our children. What could be more tragic, more senseless? Life is a clock without hands. It's always ticking, but we never know how much time we have left.

Existence seems to be a comedy of meaningless pain. We are trapped in a body that aches, bleeds, grows old, dies and decays. The body, itself, is a cruel tyrant demanding constant care and attention. From the body's tiresome demands and irritating complaints there is no escape. The state of our bodies is always a worry. Keeping them in good repair requires time and effort. The stomach is a despot. The bowel an embarrassment. The penis and the vagina a pair of sex-crazed dictators that give us anguish and ecstasy in equal measure. Our bodies are a perpetual source of humiliation and shame. They fart at inappropriate times. They leave skid marks in our drawers. They cut us down to size. They injure our dignity and our pride.

We turn away from these unpleasant truths, distract ourselves with the things that are supposed to bring us happiness. Money, love, the quest for power, fame and the admiration of our fellow sufferers. We strive for material success and are always disappointed no matter if we succeed or fail. We find success is not all it's cracked up to be. The reality can never live up to the dream. Failure, on the other hand, is a crushing blow to our self-esteem, clear evidence that we just didn't have what it takes. Either way the reward for our efforts is a profound disappointment in the fundamental structure of existence. We can't understand why life is so unfair. We know in our hearts that if we were the architects of creation we'd have organised things rather better.

The fear of death is at the root of all our anxieties. Desire is at the root of all our dissatisfaction and unhappiness. We are driven by our wants, the acquisition of things that always promise more than they deliver. When the new car arrives we sniff the leather seats, decide we need a bigger house, better furniture, a higher social status, more of everything. Each new toy, every expensive luxury, brings only momentary satisfaction before those gnawing desires return with a sharper bite. In all of us there is a hunger, an empty hole that can never be filled with the trivial objects of desire. Something else is needed.

Enter God. The perfect solution to the riddle of life. The story of Adam and Eve's expulsion from the Garden of Eden explains it all. Adam is a lazy, dim-witted young fellow, contented in his idleness, but he is lonely. God, in his kindly way, rips out one of Adam's ribs and creates an alluring female companion called Eve. We all know what happens next. They eat from the forbidden tree of knowledge and are tossed out of Eden on their ear. God, it seems, frowns on higher education. The disobedient couple find themselves in the fallen world, a vale of tears, or what Carlyle called The Hall of Doom. Here they must work, suffer and die. Here we must all work, suffer and die. That is our punishment for the Original Sin, for disobeying God's order to keep our hands off that accursed apple.

God, however, didn't abandon us completely. That would have been no fun. Like the slippery operator he is, God offered us a loophole. If we were good and obeyed his commands we could get back to the garden and enjoy everlasting life. On the other hand, if we were bad we were sentenced to an eternity of torment in a terrible place called Hell. Hell is a particularly fiendish invention. One might suspect that the Spirit in the Sky has a taste for sadism.

Religion of whatever brand offers mankind a shining hope, a system to live by and the protection of a community. But it gives him far more than that. It reduces the terror of the unknown, explains the unexplainable and provides meaning to lives that are often sad, miserable and unfulfilled.

The panacea of religion worked pretty well for a couple of thousand years. Then the Enlightenment came along and God began to lose his footing in the minds of men. Doubts about his very existence set in. The Heavenly City started to topple.

Ideas are dangerous things. They are like drops of acid burning away our comforting certainties, making holes in the fabric of our most cherished beliefs. The discoveries of science pulled God down from his throne. Dr Copernicus proved that the earth was just an insignificant pebble rolling aimlessly around a minor star, and not the very centre of the universe that we formerly supposed. Then Charles Darwin stepped into the ring and delivered the knock-out punch. He concluded that mankind had evolved from some slimy, worm-like thing wriggling up from the primeval ooze. He told us we were not the sublime creation of an all-powerful God, but a set of random mutations. Even Darwin himself shrank from this odious discovery for he realised the terrible damage it would do to the human psyche.

"God is dead!" Fredrick Nietzsche cried triumphantly as the old tyrant with a thousand names was carried from the ring.

Nietzsche spoke too soon. God is making a comeback and he's come back angry. In the Middle East millions of God-crazed fanatics with bombs and Kalashnikovs are busy slaughtering infidels in the interest of creating a better world. In the United States, God is still a hot ticket. The Christian right are tirelessly beavering away to bring back that old time religion that used to burn witches and other evil-doers at the stake. Science and religion are still locked in a deadly struggle for supremacy. Science has logic or its side. God, on the other hand, has a muscular brute called

Faith. My money is on the brute. It is easier to believe than it is to think.

Without God mankind is right back where he started, in the Vale of Tears, walking the dark Halls of Doom in a world without meaning. Science and its prodigal offspring, technology, have brought us wonderful things the old God so thoughtlessly withheld. We have all sorts of miraculous devises designed to make life easier and more carefree. Every advertisement on TV encourages us to buy something we don't need by holding up the product as a symbol of something we really do want. Youth, beauty, health, love, status, freedom. And yet all this manufactured junk doesn't make us happy. We are greedy, insatiable creatures, full of envy and spite, the true children of Original Sin. We chafe and struggle against the limitations the world imposes. We long for immortality, but can't stand an afternoon alone in our own company without going mad with boredom. We rush about on trivial pursuits in a frantic effort to mask our disappointment and unhappiness. Underneath all this frenzied activity the ancient anxiety still lurks. What sort of God would summon us into life only to gleefully subject us to such evils as fear, sickness, age, loss, labour, sorrow, strife, pain, hunger, cold? There is something chilling and malevolent in such a God.

Yet death, without God to save us, really is

death. There will be no life everlasting, no joyous family reunions with our deceased loved-ones in an untroubled heaven. All that awaits is the terrifying blackness of eternity. It is unlikely mankind will ever find a completely satisfying answer to the poignant enigma. What are we doing here? What does it all mean? Do we live and die like insects, for nothing? Nothing? Has fate decreed it so?

6

IS AN AFTERLIFE POSSIBLE?

DEATH IS NOT a popular topic at the dinner table. It's not a popular topic anywhere, except at the undertakers. The certainty of death is terrifying. The process of death is terrifying. The way most people handle the terror is not to think about death, pretend it's not waiting around the corner with a lipless grin. Humanity has gone to great lengths to deny death. We find it hard to deal with the fact of our utter disappearance into nothingness as if we never lived, dreamed, hoped, loved, suffered and sacrificed. Not only gone, but in time totally forgotten. Even on our death bed we refuse to believe this grim truth.

Doctor, doctor, please have a look.
My brow is fevered, my genitals cook.
Doctor, doctor, what can I do?
My ears they ooze a greenish goo.
Doctor, doctor, what's to be done?
My legs won't move, my bowels run.
Doctor, doctor, tell for true,
Observe my feet, that sticky dew.
Doctor, doctor, what is it you see?
That wriggling worm, did it come from me?

Doctor, Doctor, how long have I got?
Below the chin I'm starting to rot.
Doctor, doctor, how foul you smell.
It can't be me, I'm getting well!

The body dies. It dies in spite of our howls of protest and cowardly denials. The rock outlives the flower and the oak outlives the man. Life vanishes while the senseless objects endure. Buildings outlast their architects, the brush outlasts the artist and the pen outlasts the writer. The very pavements on which we walk have a much longer life than us. Creation destroys what it makes with complete indifference.

Attitudes towards death vary widely. The ancient Greeks didn't deny death. Instead, they put the emphasis on life. Death to them was a shadowy, miserable continuation of existence without any joy or fun. The gloomy Egyptians were obsessed by death. They put their efforts into building great temples of death and preserving corpses, believing a body was necessary in the next life. The Jews are more realistic. They accept death. The Buddhists yearn for death, which they call Nirvana, perfect peace. The Christians scoff at death, choosing to believe that it's a wonderful thing, the gateway to an afterlife of eternal bliss. Our own era chooses to repress the whole idea of death. Instead of allowing death to become an incentive to life we sweep it under the carpet. But that doesn't stop the fear. Death takes on a kind of stealthy, illegal existence. It jumps out of the dark to terrify us when we least expect it.

Theologians and philosophers have devised a get-out clause to escape the death sentence. It's called the soul. Definitions of the soul, just what it is, are rather vague. The theologians and the philosophers get into a terrible tangle every time they try to explain it. So they attempt to define it by explaining what the soul is not. We know it's not a material thing. It has no mass. It's invisible and undetectable, even more insubstantial than a ghost. Yet it is supposed to be an integral part of us, the only part that survives the death of the body. It is associated not with the brain, but with something called the 'mind'. Another nebulous concept. Soul and mind are basically the same thing. If it's true that we do have a soul, and that it lives on after death, what sort of life does it have? Where does it live? In heaven, floating around on a cloud? Or in hell getting roasted on a spit? It's hard to see what difference it makes. Without a body, pleasure and happiness would be severely limited. And the so-called fires of hell would have no effect. What if heaven and hell don't exist, what then? Where does the soul find a home?

The problems of the soul don't end there. Is the soul us, a sort of disembodied doppelganger? Does it have our memories, our personalities, our desires, our likes and dislikes, our good points and our bad? All the unique characteristics that make us, us and nobody else. What if the soul only takes the good things with it? Only happy memories, only the sunny side of our personalities, leaving behind the bad things like carnal desires, dislikes and our shadow side. If that's the case, then it wouldn't really be us. It would only be half us, and that would make us someone else. When the soul leaves the body it loses its home, the ability to act or to change anything, and perhaps even its identity. How could a soul even think without a brain? The idea of drifting aimlessly around the cosmos like a homeless tramp with amnesia seems a pretty grim sort of afterlife.

If you don't examine the idea of a soul too closely it's a genuinely comforting notion. Faith gives us strength. Faith gives us the courage to carry on in the teeth of grueling hardship. It keeps us from falling into utter despair when the world seems like a black hole with no bottom. The belief in an afterlife holds the terror at bay, convinces us that all the suffering and unhappiness that goes along with living won't have been for nothing. That life, indeed, has meaning. That there will be some reward at the end of it all.

Faith and reason seldom agree. Faith says: "If I believe it, it must be true." Reason stares back with contempt and says: "Show me the evidence." Alas, there is no evidence for the soul. Only conjecture and hope. Without the soul to float heavenward the possibility of an afterlife dissolves like cigarette smoke into thin air. And the terror won't go away.

God, heaven, the soul and religion itself was built on the terror of death. Animals have no religion. They worship at no shrine because death has no meaning for them. They aren't afraid of it because they aren't aware of it. Only human beings are aware of death. Nature has bestowed this curse on its most sophisticated creation as a consequence of our self-awareness and our ability to draw conclusions from our observations. Human beings are clever, clever enough to invent fictions that will comfort and soothe the uneasy mind. I fear the soul is just such a fiction.

What if it's all just bullshit? That there is no God, no heaven, and no afterlife? What if our existence really is meaningless, a strange, inexplicable accident without reason or purpose? That is the existentialist view. They point out that the onus is on us to provide the meaning. Human beings have a powerful hunger to believe in something larger than themselves. A creed, a sturdy tree to hang on to throughout the storm we call life. Religion is one tree. There are many to choose from. Politics, art, science, money-making, nationalism, race and family are others. Cults and mass movements are also popular, particularly among failures, misfits, minorities and sinners seeking redemption. But these are just substitutes, a way of distracting us from the supressed terror of death. Only God has the remedy. Only religion offers us a way out, an answer to the great riddle of life. People of faith are the happiest and most untroubled. Nothing can pry them loose from their chosen tree. The rest of us grasp at twigs and are tossed around in the storm to find shelter where we can.

Atheists and non-believers pay a penalty for their scepticism. They must face death naked, stripped of all illusions and comforting fairy tales.

The hero and the heroine are the ones who have entered the kingdom of death and come back alive, the survivors of war, the firefighters who dash into a burning house to save a child, the witch doctor who braves the spirit world to drive illness away. The world's myths are filled with heroic characters who have descended into the underworld to accomplish some mission for the benefit of mankind. Alas, most of us are not heroes standing tall and strong in our nakedness, staring death in the face and spitting in his eye. We shiver and cringe in our nakedness, beg for mercy and mumble a prayer just in case, against all the odds, a merciful God really does exist.

There is one final ray of hope. Perhaps life here on earth is merely a dream. It seems real, but is not. Our real self exists in another dimension somewhere absorbing our dream memories and experiences as they happen. Could it be that death is only a waking up from this dream of life? That our dream-selves rise at death to join our real selves in an entirely different place outside of time and earthly suffering?

Whenever I think of death I think of Joseph Stalin in his Kremlin office at three o'clock in the morning. His finger is running down a list of names. The finger arbitrarily stops at a certain name, a person he has never heard of and has no grudge against. Uncle Joe smiles and reaches for the phone. That person is innocently unaware that doom is coming. He expects to wake up and drink a cup of coffee. It comes as a terrible shock to discover that he won't live to see daylight.

Death is an awfully big adventure. That's the way I look at it. I'm old. My bags are packed and I'm ready to go. I can't say I'm looking forward to the trip. But a part of me is curious to know what lies behind the veil that separates life from death. Will all be revealed? Or will it just be darkness and oblivion?

7

Is Evil Really So Bad?

EVIL IS A snake with two heads. One head is natural evil, that is to say volcanoes, earthquakes, hurricanes, floods, disease, aging and death, all the terrible things that brutal bitch, Mother Nature, throws at us without a hint of mercy. The other head is human evil, the terrible things we do to each other without a hint of mercy. Together these two evils have made life on this planet hellish at times.

The problem of evil is a serious stumbling block to the belief in God. If God exists why does he allow it? Maybe God isn't merciful or even good. Perhaps he is like the old gods of Greece, a mixture of good and evil similar to us humans. Or maybe God is powerless to prevent evil. If that is the case, then he is impotent, a limp-dick deity unworthy of worship. If he can prevent evil, but chooses not to do so, then he is malevolent and equally unworthy of worship. In any case an arrest warrant should be issued. God should be hauled down to the courthouse and tried for crimes against humanity.

So much needless pain. So much wanton suffering. So much misery, anguish and despair. And we are helpless. There are no remedies for these evils. We are the playthings of chance and fate. The two great symbols of human existence are Tantalus, who was doomed to go hungry and thirsty while sitting beside a bubbling brook under a nourishing fruit tree. Like the rest of us, Tantalus was tormented by maddening desires that would never be satisfied. The other great symbol is Sisyphus, condemned to roll a great stone endlessly to the top of a hill only for it to roll back down when he reached the top demonstrating the futility of desire, the meaninglessness of life. No wonder so many are undone by the irrational cruelty of it all.

Arthur Schopenhauer, the gloomiest of philosophers, believed the problem of evil was so dire that it was a blessing to die in infancy, or even better, not to have been born at all. He defined existence in negatives. Pleasure was the absence of pain. Good the absence of evil. And he had some convincing arguments to back up his negativity. Take one animal eating another. Isn't the pain of the eaten greater than the pleasure of the eater? For Schopenhauer, ours is the worst of all possible worlds. He thought human life shouldn't exist. This towering pessimist paved the way for Nihilism, the blackest of doctrines, which finds pleasure in absolutely nothing.

The existentialists lightened things up a bit. They knew life was a pointless, grim affair, but what the hell, let's kick up our heels and party. Why not tango to the music melancholy? Why not squeeze some fun out of this bitter fruit? Since life is meaningless, it is up to us to create meaning for ourselves. It doesn't matter what that meaning is, or its effects on others so long as it provides a reason for getting up in the morning.

This sensible, pragmatic approach makes the Devil smile. He knows the havoc billions of self-serving humans will bring. The selfishness, the intolerance, the cruelty and the chaos caused by the competition for meaning of one individual against another, or one group against another. Fascism versus democracy. Communism versus capitalism. Christianity versus Islam. Blacks versus whites. Women versus men. We see it today under the umbrella name of Political Correctness. Satan surely loves Political Correctness.

The notion that God is evil isn't a pleasant thought. No major religion supports this view, although the God of the Old Testament comes pretty close. Perhaps God is all powerful, but not too bright, a lord with learning difficulties. Or maybe he's just lazy and can't be bothered to answer our prayers. Or maybe he falls asleep on the job. None of these excuses, or any other loophole dreamed up by heaven's attorneys, are very satisfying. A real villain is needed.

Enter the Devil, the prince of darkness, the lord of the flies, ruler of the bottomless pit – the Evil One. Satan, of course, lets God off the hook. God isn't to blame for the roof tile falling on Daddy's head, or the baby drowned in the paddling pool, or the nun raped and strangled with her rosary. That was all the Devil's work. Existence is a titanic struggle between good and evil, between light and darkness, between ignorance and enlightenment, between order and chaos.

Satan brings drama into the world. Without him there would be no stories, no literature, no myths, no comic book superheroes, nothing to fight against and overcome. There would be no battles, no sacrifices, no saints, no need for courage and determination. The world would be a bland, unexciting place, like a cut-rate amusement park without the rides, a horrifying glimpse of heaven. Satan brings a lot to the table. Good isn't possible without evil. White needs black for contrast. Neither can exist without the other. The world is built on duality. Most everything has its opposite number. God needs Satan every bit as much as Satan needs God.

Atheists have no use for this scenario. They toss both God and Satan into the trash can, along with hell and heaven. Philosophy claims evil is merely the absence of good. Science explains that natural evil is the price we pay for living in a universe that conforms to the laws of physics. Enlightened thinkers tell us human evil is a social problem that can be cured with the correct applications. Exactly what these applications are is a matter of violent debate. Riots in the leafy groves of academia. Some advocate therapy, a huggy-kissy approach with the emphasis on sympathy and understanding. Others recommend mind-altering drugs, particularly for children who demonstrate an independence of spirit. Still others want more prisons, longer sentences and lethal injections. All have been tried and none have made a dint in the problem of evil. Free will isn't so easily stamped out. Evil stubbornly flourishes like Japanese knotweed in our green and blue garden.

One solution to the problem of evil is to deny that evil exists. The Hindus believe evil is an illusion. In the United States it is the central dogma of Christian Science. This idea can be traced all the way back to Plato. (Is there any idea that can't be traced back to Plato)? Evil is the absence of good. The further we stray from God the darker the world becomes. Or to put it another way, the more we put our own selfish interests above the common good the larger the shadow looms.

The Hindus and the Christian Scientists are kidding themselves. Who can watch the evening news and deny the existence of evil? It is there in the bloody slaughter in the Ukraine. It is there in the offices of high government officials planning their next drone strike, or plotting to over-throw a foreign government of which they disapprove. It is there in the board rooms of the big banks devising new ways to swindle the public. It is there every time a suicide bomber kills innocent people. It is there every time a woman is raped, a wife beaten, a child murdered, an animal tortured. It is there with dripping jaws. And Satan is a happy bunny.

Is it possible that evil is a punishment for all the bad things we've done in a previous existence? Could it be that the earth is, in fact, hell? That we've been sent here to atone. This is the Buddhist view of life. For the Buddhist desire is at the root of all evil. Kill desire and human evil will die. But so will joy, love, fun and all the other things that make living bearable. We are strapped to the wheel of recurrent existences, doomed to be born and to suffer over and over again, like some nightmarish Groundhog Day, until we get it right and are allowed to expire into absolute nothingness. If that were true I'd put a bullet in my head. Then

I'd be reborn a worm and have to start all over again working my way up the evolutionary scale. Even suicide is no solution.

I don't find evil in the least bit shocking. What shocks me is goodness. There is so little kindness in the world that when I encounter it I'm left gobsmacked. Back in 1986 I faced a family emergency. My father was living in a retirement home in California and they were kicking him out because he'd gotten too sick and feeble to look after himself. What my father needed was a nursing home with full time care. That was something I couldn't afford. So I flew out to LA to bring dad back home to London to live with me and my family. This was at Christmas time. The old man was in bad shape, crippled up with Parkinson's disease and a host of other health problems. On Boxing Day we boarded a flight to Newark, New Jersey, where we to catch a connecting flight to London. When we landed disaster struck. Something evil happened. The airline we'd booked for London had gone out of business. There we were stranded in Newark, New Jersey, in the bleak mid-winter among an angry crowd of passengers all demanding explanations. We were told there would be no flights until the next morning. I looked at the old man, shaking and frail in his wheelchair. I could see he was all in. He needed his medicine, a hot meal and a good night's sleep. It was freezing outside and snowing. I managed to get a cab to one of the hotels near the airport. When I got inside with the old man and a ton of luggage, the desk clerk informed me that no rooms were available. The hotel was full. I pointed to the old man, pleaded with the desk clerk to find us a bed. He called around to all the other hotels. Every hotel was full. There wasn't a room to be had. The clerk said we were welcome to stay in the lobby. The lobby was jammed. Every seat was taken. I didn't think the old man was going to make it through the night. Just then, at my lowest point, a stranger touched my arm. "You can have my room," he said, handing me his key. I just stared at him. I couldn't believe my ears. He wanted nothing for it, no reward, or compensation. It was an act of kindness, of simple human goodness.

That's not just a heart-warming Christmas tale. It's one small example of good growing from something evil. Whenever I despair of the human race, which is often, I think of that man, that Good Samaritan, and my spirit lifts a little. Every act of kindness, every generous offer, every good deed, every unselfish gesture slaps the smirk off Satan's face and lets a chink of sunlight into this dark old world. Sometimes the light hurts our eyes, but it's an illuminating hurt.

Is evil really so bad, or is it a variant of good dressed up in a black disguise?

PART THREE

Yang and Yin: The Clash of Opposites

8

US VERSUS THEM

THERE IS A crack in what God has made. A deep, impassable fissure runs through the heart of creation. On opposite sides are light and darkness, good and evil, war and peace, love and hate, sickness and health, beauty and ugliness, happiness and despair, famine and plenty, winners and losers. It seems everything is in conflict with everything else, a Thomas Hobbs world of all against all. A profound, inexpungable discord appears to govern the cosmos. The universe is unquestionably at war with itself. Creation displays a split personality: kindly and cruel, generous and inhuman. If God is in evidence so is the Devil. They are competing brothers in the enterprise of life.

Why this antagonism in the very core of creation? Some believe it is part of the plan and actually works to our advantage. That it might even be a necessary condition of existence. If this disharmony could be abolished the universe would certainly disappear. Movement implies resistance. Up implies down, right implies left, light implies dark. If there was no liking, how could there be disliking? If there was no east there is no west. Without cold there is no heat. To feel always the same is not to feel at all. Without this struggle of opposing forces life would be an intolerable monotony. Nothing would take place. The world would sink into motiveless, motionless stagnation. The busy, bustling life we knew gone. Nothing but boredom and idleness.

This clash of opposites could have given birth to the universe. From this collision of mighty forces the world has arisen in all its beauty, ugliness and contradictions. We ourselves are schizophrenic beings, children born in the dark soil of conflict. Without contraries there is no progression. Attraction and repulsion, reason and irrationality, love and hate are necessary to human existence.

Not everyone thinks that way. Some prefer to take the path of retreat. The life-hating sages of the east retire in disgust from the frenzied business of the world. This sense of defeatism comes to full flower in Indian philosophy. They conjecture the love of life is at the root of all evil. Destroy it and you're half-way to heaven. The wise man shrinks away from the conflict. Escape is the goal. These sages, like the stoics after them, seek a passionless impassivity that will free them from desire, love, pleasure and pain. They live under a tree, surrendering all things, tasting neither grief nor happiness, utterly indifferent to the life around them. Indian philosophers are metaphysicians. Everything is an illusion, Maya, deception. Apathy allows the emancipated soul into Brahma where all earthly concerns melt away. Where no joys, sorrows or troubles can intrude. Nothing but unrelieved serenity. A kind of living death.

The Chinese chose another path. For centuries the life of China was guided by the ideas of Confucius. He was a realist. To him the business of the world was important. Earthly life and the ordering of its affairs and social structures were paramount concerns. He believed something practical could be done to mitigate the inevitable afflictions heaped upon the human race. Confucius says: "Think first of today and how it best can be spent. Much is possible." Or, "Good manners are not to be despised and a good temper helps ease the frictions of social intercourse." As a result of this practical outlook the Chinese developed paper, woodblock printing, porcelain and competitive written examinations for public servants. They also invented gunpowder, but sensibly only used it for fireworks.

The Chinese take pleasure in the world. They appreciate beauty. They are connoisseurs of delicate flavours and evanescent perfumes. They recognise the charm of elegance, of style, the pleasure to be derived from music and verse, or the shape of a vase. A lovely flower, an exquisite face, a choice tea, the touch of a fabric, all have value.

China wasn't blind to the warring duality in nature. To these mighty, opposing forces she gave the names Yang and Yin. Yang is youth, health, summer, warmth and sunshine. Yin is old age, ill-health, winter, dark and cold. Alternatively, they manifest themselves in the ebb and flow of sap in the trees. Yang comes with spring and summer, Yin with autumn and winter. Neither can exist alone. In the human sphere of thought and action, Yang is growth, joy, honour, profit and fame. Yin is decay, loss, distress, misery and ignorance.

The human race needs a spur. It requires resistance, enemies to defeat, obstacles to overcome, problems to solve. As Nietzsche said. "What doesn't kill me makes me stronger." He advocated the hard mountain path. An effortless existence is not found in nature. Life isn't about avoiding issues, fleeing encounters, resting in cradled comfort, or cowering in a corner. Such people might be as good as gold and fit for heaven, but they are useless on earth. The love of life and the hatred of life are the two great moods of the human heart.

9

Opposing Ideologies

Democracy is an ancient dream. It was born almost overnight in Athens during the fifth century BC. Such a political experiment had never been tried before. It ushered something new into the world. Before that there were pharaohs, kings, tyrants and emperors. Democracy is very different. It is a political system that believes in freely-elected government and representative assemblies which guarantee the rule of law, including citizens' rights and freedom of speech, publication and assembly. It was based on the values of reason, public debate, education, science and the improvability of the human condition. The key notes here are personal freedom and economic prosperity. In these two areas democracy has been wildly successful in spite of the inherent greed and corruption built into the system which lead to the cyclical financial crashes and the devastation that follows.

Modern democracy was born in blood. It came in on the back of religious toleration. The Reformation had ignited a mad wave of religious hatred. Protestants and Catholics had been battling it out, fiercely trying to exterminate one another for a hundred years. This ended with the horror of the thirty-years war. When it was all over both sides, utterly exhausted, looked around and saw the balance between the contending parties was about the same as it was before all this unnecessary destruction and bloodshed. By the seventieth century sanity had returned and it was agreed that people should be allowed to believe what they want.

Religious toleration came to England with the Dutch King William along with the Bank of England and the national debt. The most astute advocate of liberty at that time was John Locke, the founding father of philosophical liberalism. His ideas of government are deeply imbedded in the American constitution, as well as in those of Britain and France. Locke's mind was focused on the problem of reconciling the maximum of freedom to the minimum of government. Political thinkers are still puzzling it out to this day.

Democracy came to full flower in the nineteenth century. Personal freedom, a free press, free speech and freedom from arbitrary arrest was taken for granted, at least in the western democracies. The architects of democracy knew that government can exist without laws, but laws can't exist without government. The democratic system was invented to reconcile government with liberty. Without government there can be no such thing as civilization. History clearly shows that any group of people entrusted with power will abuse that power if they can get away with it. Democracy limits power, by making it temporary, by holding elections at regular intervals.

Democracy is far from perfect and has its limitations. It is economically unfair. It tends toward a tyranny of the majority and the suppression and persecution of minorities. It promotes conformity and frowns on the unconventional. Freedom of the press is not open to doctrines thought to be dangerously subversive. Free speech doesn't allow recommending the assassination of unpopular politicians, or people who disagree with you. Democracy, like every other political system, is human and open to all sorts of abuses. Yet despite all its failures and flaws democracy has proved to be one of the better ideas that have helped the human race. One might call it the political Yang.

10

COMMUNISM

COMMUNISM, LIKE DEMOCRACY, was born in blood and passionate hope for a better life. Revolutionary movements despise the present and always look forward to a shining future. They generate exuberance and wild expectations that are seldom met. Communism attempted to build a proletarian Utopia, a worker's paradise where everyone was equal and would share equally in the benefits of their collective labour. From each according to his ability, to each according to his need. Men would become brothers. Experts would plan the organization of this brave new world. Technology would tame unruly nature, labour would make the workers free. (This very slogan adorned the entrance to Nazi death camps}. Life would be one long, wonderful summer's day.

The Communist dream appealed to the poor and the oppressed all over the world. And not only to the poor and oppressed. Western intellectuals, writers, artists, radicals and social reformers flocked to the new Soviet Union and returned home dazzled to praise this humanitarian miracle.

In order to create such a miracle, four things were necessary. Belief in the dream, determination, commitment and self-sacrifice, especially self-sacrifice. Most people would prefer to sacrifice their next-door neighbour rather than themselves. To ripen a person for self-sacrifice they must first be stripped of their identity, cease to be an individual, an autonomous being with an existence bounded by birth and death. The best way to achieve this is by assimilation into the group. The assimilated person does not see himself and others as human beings, but as a member of a tribe, or a family. He or she has no worth or purpose beyond the aims of the group. The group offers a kind of immortality. As long as the group exists he cannot die.

Why did such a noble experiment fail? Economics was a major factor. The only saleable commodities the undeveloped Soviet Union produced were fossil fuels, vodka, caviar and those sinister Russian dolls that fit inside each other. The rest of their manufactured goods was junk.

The techniques used for mobilizing resources was backward and the performance shoddy. Small, primitive, unreliable automobiles cost a fortune and took years to deliver. When they finally arrived no spare parts were available. Electrical appliances were at the mercy of frequent power failures and blackouts. Apartment buildings were surrounded by nets to keep the crumbling masonry from killing pedestrians. Empty shops, long queues and lack of public services was the reality in the worker's paradise. Only the privileged party elite had access to the special stores stuffed with foreign luxuries. The Soviet elite, like all elites, lived comfortably above the long-suffering proletariat. Equality was a myth, a fairy tale. This was the dirty secret of Soviet communism.

Another major factor in the Soviet collapse was indifference. Nothing worked and nobody cared. The Communist system produced only ugliness. Everything was slipshod. Nothing functioned properly. Buildings were made of raw cement blocks and windows were out of true. The infrastructure was crumbling, equipment broken down heaps of rusting machinery piled outside the grim factories. There was a joke shared by the people waiting in the long queues. "We'll pretend we've worked and Uncle Joe will pretend he's paid." The deceived Soviet citizens huddled in their cold, tiny flats and drowned their disappointments in an ocean of vodka.

When the Soviet premier, Nikita Khrushchev, flew to California to meet with the American president, John F. Kennedy, it was said that he glanced out the aeroplane window and asked what those patches of blue were in the backyards of houses.

"Swimming pools," he was told.

A look of horror spread across the premier's face. He could hardly believe that ordinary people enjoyed such luxury, that Capitalism could produce such an abundance of wealth. At that terrible moment he realized the Communist system was doomed to disappear like the dinosaur. And so it proved. Soviet Communism didn't die a violent death. It died like a sick old man that had cheated and lied to his family. Communism lost its legitimacy. The dream vanished. The wall came down and the family walked out to leave the old tyrant to a lingering death.

11

MODERNISM

WHEN PEOPLE SAY the word 'modern' what they are really referring to is the enlightenment that began in the 17th century and continues in some degree to this very day. Never before in human history had mankind taken such a giant leap forward in material and social progress and in the understanding of the world around him. The enlightenment gave us religious toleration, democracy, capitalism, human rights, the scientific method, the industrial revolution and a dominance over nature itself. It harnessed the dreaded power of lightning, turned electricity into energy that lights and fuels our planet. Astronomy gave us a new and disturbing picture of reality and upset our cosy notions about the universe and our place in it. The enlightenment figured out how money and the market actually worked. It brought a heady spirit of optimism and the promise of a bright future. It produced Newton, Kepler, Galileo, Voltaire, Locke, Mill, Ben Franklin, Adam Smith and a host of others. The enlightenment was an age of genius, a time of discovery.

Before the enlightenment European thought was dominated by two unchallenged authorities: scripture and the classics. However great were the classical authors, the one unquestionable voice of knowledge and duty was the voice of God as recorded in the Bible. The Old Testament contained both the history of the human race and the explanation of God's purpose. Nothing else was needed or wanted. The authority of the Bible was absolute. The medieval mind was tormented by demons and superstitious terrors. The 16th and early 17th centuries were a time of the great witch hunts, when thousands were being burned at the stake for sorcery and compacts with the devil. Life for most was a gruelling struggle for survival. The church taught that the sufferings and hardships and injustice of this world were but a preparation for heaven and eternal happiness would be your reward.

These teachings were severely undermined by the achievements of science. It proved that life didn't have to be nasty, brutish and short. The products of science went a long way to mitigating the sufferings of humanity. Science brought pain relief, an increased life span, labour-saving machinery, greater material comfort, economic prosperity and the promise of an even better future. There was no longer any need for God. Man was now the master of his own destiny. Human intelligence had no use for the supporting arm of theology to find its way to the truth. The teachings in the Bible were becoming increasing hard to defend.

The underlying power of science was human reason. Reason was responsible for all the new-found abundance and wealth. The enlightenment elevated reason above everything else. It was described as a candle in the dark, a fragment of the divine and nature's greatest gift to man. Reason allowed us to penetrate to the world's deepest secrets. It gave us civilization. It freed us from ignorance and superstition and pointed the way forward to a sunny tomorrow. Reason ascended the throne of thought and was worshipped as a benevolent god.

12

THE ROMANTICS

GODS DO NOT go unchallenged. The backlash came with the Romantic Movement. The previous generation, the men of the enlightenment, had vivid recollections of the calamitous wars of religion and the vicious civil wars in England, France and Germany. They saw first-hand the terror of anarchy and chaos, the barbarous destruction that comes with the unleashing of irrational passions. The men of the enlightenment recognised the importance of safety and the sacrifices necessary to achieve it. Prudence was highly valued. Reason was the most effective weapon against the mob and social madness. Newton's orderly, law-abiding cosmos became the symbol of good government. The restraint of primitive instincts became the aim of education. The enlightenment provided a tranquillity so ridged, so dead, and so hostile to an adventurous life that nobody but nervous old men could endure it.

The romantics had no use for reason. They preferred raw emotion to social restraint, rural landscapes to crowded cities, Gothic architecture to classical Greek. They revelled in wildness rather than tameness. They enjoyed raging storms, fearful precipices, pathless forests and tempests at sea. They loved what is useless, destructive and violent. This is best reflected in their fiction. They dwelled on what was creepy and strange: ghosts, ghouls, vampires, dead bodies, crypts, ancient decaying castles, the last melancholy descendants of once great families, madness, mesmerism and the occult arts. The romantics didn't want peace, quiet and safety. They wanted action and danger, a vigorous individual life.

They were also preoccupied with beauty. Utility didn't matter. Aesthetics was what really counted. The tiger is beautiful, but not useful. The earthworm is useful, but not beautiful. Darwin, no romantic, praised the earthworm. Blake, who was a romantic, praised the tiger.

Because the romantic outlook was aristocratic and because it preferred passion to calculation it was a vehement opponent of commerce and finance. Capitalism was the enemy. The romantic's hatred of capitalism was quite different from socialist hatred. The socialists were on the side of the proletariat. The romantics thought money-making merely vulgar, a contemptable activity dominated by Jews. The Romantic Movement never challenged reason effectively, but it signalled rebellion was in the wind.

13

POSTMODERNISM: THE COUNTER-ENLIGHTENMENT

THE FIRST SERIOUS challenge to reason came from Germany. The man who led the charge was Immanuel Kant, a retiring, unmarried philosopher who passed his whole, uneventful, life in the town of Konigsberg in East Prussia. Kant didn't believe in frivolities. He allowed only one picture in his small house. It was a picture of Jean Jacques Rousseau, the founder of the Romantic Movement (more on him later). Kant greatly admired Rousseau's work, but was more religious than romantic. He was troubled by the beating religion had taken at the hands of the enlightenment thinkers. He realized that religion could not be justified rationally. One or the other had to go. Kant decided to knock reason off its pedestal, to destroy its credibility. He attempted this in his famous book *The Critique of Pure Reason*. In the preface he stated his aim clearly: "I found it necessary to deny knowledge in order to make room for faith." Kant identified five features essential to reason: objectivity, competence, autonomy, universality and mental power. He realised objectivity was the most important. If that fell the rest would follow.

Kant knew for reason to be objective it must connect with reality. The only way to do that is through the senses. The information is then internalised, erecting a barrier between reality and reason. A man looks at a rose and sees the colour red. His wife looks at that same rose and believes it to be pink. Who is right? What is the real colour of the rose? It is impossible to say objectively. An orange tastes sweet. But eat a spoonful of honey first and the orange tastes sour. Which is it? Sweet or sour? If reason is not directly aware of reality, then the observable, material world vanishes, becomes something to be inferred and inaccessible to reason. This is greatly simplifying Kant's argument, but it points to the fact that reason was vulnerable and easy to attack.

Kant's book was influential and widely read. It

opened the door to all sorts of questions. Shakespeare said it best. "There is nothing either good or bad, but thinking makes it so." This seems to be the truth. When one looks back at the past, or at the present moment, one is forced to ask if enlightenment had put a false god on the throne of thought? When did reason ever control human affairs? What chance does reasoned debate have against a frenzied mob filled with the passion of a holy cause? If logic was the guiding light then why do revolutions that start in the name of reason end up in blood and slaughter? "When the people undertake to reason," Voltaire said, "all is lost." Humans soon become weary of reasoned argument and resort to quicker measures to settle a disagreement. A bullet in the head usually does the trick.

Thoughts are swirling around all the time, but who believes where there is universal freedom there is also universal intelligence? Who believes where there is education there is good sense? Who believes representative government brings equality and justice? Reason is a prejudice of the mind. Was Christ rational? Was Mahomet? What about Luther and Robespierre? Were Hitler and Stalin rational? Opinions differ. Human thinking, high and low, is worm-eaten with prejudice and fallacy. That was the counter-enlightenment view.

Reason might be easily attacked, but it wasn't

easily defeated. By the 1950's the left had grown desperate. The whole ideology was in crisis. The left had been beaten by reason and the political right on every front. Classical Marxism makes four major claims. 1. Capitalism exploits the poor and enriches the wealthy. That it is brutally competitive and thus unfair both domestically and internationally. 2. Socialism by contrast is humane and peaceful. It promotes sharing, equality and cooperation. 3. Capitalism is morally corrupt. Since the rich get richer and poor get poorer, the class conflict will bring it down. 4. Socialist economies will be more productive and create a new era of prosperity and happiness.

The left proved to be wrong on every count. The enlightenment had been spectacularly triumphant. The left had been totally discredited. Capitalism worked. Socialism's top down, command economies always failed. Every socialist experiment had been a dismal disaster from the Soviet Union and the Eastern Bloc, to Vietnam, North Korea, Cuba, Ethiopia and Mozambique. Time and time again socialism has proved to be more brutal than the worst dictatorships in history prior to the 20th century. By contrast the western democracies had a solid record of respecting individual rights and providing the means for people to build meaningful, self-determined lives. The intellectual and political left had been badly beaten and were on the ropes. The question every socialist was asking was this: should I admit defeat, or go on fighting?

14

THE FOUR HORSEMEN OF POSTMODERNISM

THE PROBLEM FACED by the postmodernists was the same problem Christianity faced in the 17th century. In both cases the evidence was against them. They were no longer taken seriously. Nobody believed the message anymore. Not people in general, not even the poor who were better off under capitalism. Despite the evidence the postmodernists could no more let go of their cherished beliefs than the Christians could stop believing in God. Drastic measures were needed.

The four horsemen who turned things around were Michel Foucault, Jacques Derrida, Jean-Francios Lyotard and Richard Rorty, three Frenchmen and an American. All were far left wing, and all were academic intellectuals, men who produce nothing but ideas, good, bad, or downright absurd. In the case of the four horsemen their ideas were at the absurd end of the spectrum. Foucault, for instance, wanted to abandon criminality as a category and turn all the jailed criminals loose. We see the same thing today in the movement to defund the police. We see it in contemporary California where criminals are running riot. Foucault was similar to the Marquis de Sade in that he liked to go to the limit and beyond. He wrote books about madhouses and prisons. He preached a mad philosophy to his students and followers. The core idea of the four horsemen was that logic and evidence prove nothing. Feelings are deeper than logic. Feelings are all that matter. They promote using language not as a vehicle for seeking truth, but as a rhetorical device to undermine logic and bring evidence into question. They knew that language can obscure as well as illuminate, mislead as well as guide. Language is the intellectual's tool and the four horsemen knew how to misuse it effectively. The postmodernists feel no obligation to tell the truth, only to be interesting. Truth or lies are irrelevant. What matters is effectiveness. Using language as a means of conflict resolution is not on the postmodern agenda.

It was Derrida who gave us Deconstructionism, a critical system that allows the dissembling of texts or ideas and reassembling the parts to fit any meaning or point of view the critic wishes it to have. Some texts and ideas must be thrown out because they because they are beyond the pale. Books written by dead white men are not open to redemption. Out go Shakespeare and Darwin and all the other great books of the western canon. The new canon might be vastly inferior, but anything is better than dead white men who argued reasonably with the weight of evidence on their side. Even gender has been deconstructed. Men can suddenly become women, and vice versa. Logic stands aghast.

And their lies have been very effective. Thanks to the four horsemen the left have sprung off the ropes and are battering the conservative right to the canvas. Political Correctness is now winning all the rounds. It has taken over our institutions, our media, our politicians, and our major corporations. Whether or not the people running these operations believe all this mind-numbing nonsense is a moot point. Whatever they believe they are too frightened and cowardly to stand up to the lies and the intimidation.

Academic intellectuals have been a long neglected group. Other sorts of intellectuals, those in medicine and science, have traditionally hogged all the limelight. The academics were resentful and jealous and wanted their share of recognition and respect. One way to get the recognition they craved was to drag politics into the mix. Leftist thought had dominated intellectuals in the 20th century. Before that the left had believed in the enlightenment program of evidence, reason, logic, civility, tolerance and fair play. All that started to change in the 1980's. The left became less tolerant and more aggressive. It became hostile to debate, snarled at dissent, engaged in vilification and name calling and used anger and rage against anyone they didn't agree with. How did this happen? How did the idealistic left turn into such a nasty bully?

Postmodernism is the code of the sheep, an ideology for the weakling and the underdog. The left had been bullied for two hundred years. And like all victims of abuse wanted to hit back, to wreak a devastating revenge. The left knew it couldn't attack reason directly. It had tried that and been quickly smacked down. The only real weapon the left had was words, so it turned to the dark art of propaganda. The figure of Iago springs to mind whenever I think of the postmodern personality. Iago hates Othello, but he knows he can't beat him fairly, so he strikes at what Othello loves most, Desdemona. Iago whispers in Othello's ear that his lady love is a slut who's sleeping around. These lies destroy Othello's life. He kills the woman he loves. Iago succeeds by rumor, creating suspicion and doubt and mistrust. That is the postmodernist way. Want to ruin an enemy's life, then call him a racist. Accuse him of a sex crime. It doesn't have to be true, only plausible. The same principle applies to society at large. Creating doubt, suspicion and mistrust in the prevailing order is the first step in destroying that order.

The postmodernists claim that the west is deeply racist. Yet they know the west ended slavery. They know racism is on the run but shout the opposite. They say the west is deeply sexist. Yet they know the west gave women the vote. Women in the west are the freest in the world. They argue that capitalist countries are cruel and exploit the poor. Yet they know the poor are better off in the west than in any other place on earth. The left are blatant liars and know they are liars. But they don't care. All that matters is the effectiveness of the lie.

PART FOUR

To Be or Not To Be

15

TO BE

THE WILL TO live is universal and madly insistent. Nature demonstrates it, existence manifests it, and the life of every living thing proclaims it in colour and profusion. And we know it in ourselves, the hunger for life, and the rage at death. We've won the struggle to exist. We are here. We are alive and conscious of our surroundings. That, in itself, is a miracle. I'm a miracle and so are you. But that is only the beginning of the story. Now that we've arrived on this strange, not always welcoming planet, we must go about the business of keeping alive and acquiring the means to do so. We soon discover the rules of society curb and cage us. Other people are always interfering, thwarting our designs and our desires. We must tolerate their absurd and cantankerous prejudices, cope with their meddling and overlook their annoying habits. This world is not an easy place to make a home. It is a chaotic, turbulent residence full of mad confusion, cruel injustice and terrible strife. And yet most of us choose to stay, and embrace life as we find it, not how we wish it to be.

Most people don't trouble themselves with the great metaphysical questions. Why am I here? What is the purpose of life? Why is there something rather than nothing? Does God exist? Is there an afterlife? They have more important things to do. Raising a family, earning a living, trying to get along with the neighbours and squeezing as much happiness as they can from the circumstances in which they find themselves. They take pleasure in friendships, a beautiful landscape, the sun on their naked flesh, the touch of a loved one's hand and the thousands of seemingly little things that make life worthwhile. The will to live has given us love, surely the greatest gift this life has to offer.

Human beings are not feeble souls. They know all about suffering, worry and hardship. Yet they find delight in society, in family relationships, in the sound of human voices, in convivial meetings and in the bustle, the banter and the debate all around them. The merchants of gloom and the traders in despair will find no audience among such people. The human heart wasn't built for retreat.

Nothing has ever been accomplished by resignation. All the progress of mankind has been made by people who loved the world, who had ambition, who were aggressive. Often they made huge mistakes and let loose a flood of troubles, but they moved humanity forward. They didn't regard meekness as a virtue but a contemptible and dangerous vice. There is, as Shelly says, something in man that is at enmity with dissolution and nothingness.

This race of ours has emerged from the darkness into the light and no one told us how. We have learned how to organize societies for the better or for the worse, we have built comfortable dwellings in which to live, we've developed medicines to cure illness and relieve pain, we've invented laws and a system of justice, we've transformed a wild, inhospitable planet into quite a desirable piece of real estate and no one told us how. None of this was accomplished by timid, retiring souls moaning and snivelling about the unfairness of life, who believe existence is an appalling, catastrophic blunder.

The human race can be divided into two basic types, optimists and pessimists. It seems that some people are born to be gloomy and others to be happy. I agree this is unfair. But Mother Nature is neither rational nor kind. She plays by her own rules. The Yang and the Yin of it are beyond our control. Is the decision 'to be or not to be' determined in the makeup of our DNA? Or is that too simple an explanation?

16

NOT TO BE

WHAT'S THE POINT of it all? If life has no purpose, what are we doing here? Such metaphysical questions are unanswerable. There is no use asking them. God will not reply. So, let's set such speculations aside and concentrate on a question that can be answered, individually, by every member of the human race. Is it better to be alive or dead? Opinions differ. But it seems the majority are on the side of Yang, of life. Why? Why are some people happy and others driven to put guns in their mouths? What is it about life that makes some of us want to die?

Suicide is still much frowned upon, and thought a shameful act. The coward's way out. Civilizations have outlawed it. The Catholics condemn it as a mortal sin, a one-way ticket to hell. Yet it wasn't always so. The Romans approved of suicide, even thought it praiseworthy in certain circumstances. When Petronius, author of *The Satyricon*, a biting satire on Roman society, was told the emperor, Nero, was going to order him to commit suicide, Petronius didn't wait for the order to arrive. Instead, he held a valedictory dinner party, with songs, laughter and jokes. He opened his veins and died among friends. A good death. Not everyone is so fortunate.

Approximately 800,000 people a year kill themselves. Many more than that attempt suicide. A high percentage of them will try again and succeed. They seek death for good reasons and for foolish reasons. Some do it to escape terminal disease, chronic pain, ill health, mental problems, bereavement, physical disabilities and intolerable loneliness. Others do it because of love, divorce, financial difficulties, business failures or a sudden reversal of fortune. A few do it out of spite, to punish their lover or their families. Whatever the reason, most suicides are motivated by despair. But there are exceptions. The judicial suicide that forced Socrates to drink hemlock. The ordered suicide that befell Seneca and Petronius. The spontaneous suicide, the sudden irresistible impulse to die, such as the case of the English lord who suddenly and without reason hurled himself into

Vesuvius, quickly followed by some of his companions. The heroic suicide, when a soldier throws himself on top of a grenade to save his buddies. The mass suicide of the Jews at Masada was a heroic refusal to be defeated by the Romans. The mass suicide at Jonestown was something entirely different. It was an altruistic suicide, motivated by group loyalty and the delusional thinking of a charismatic leader.

Do some of us as Freud suggested have a built-in death wish? There have been cases of people developing an overpowering desire for death. Thoughts of suicide begin to take over their mind for no reason at all. They are not depressed, or in ill health. They are not mentally unbalanced, victims of love, or with financial problems. Such cases are puzzling, both to the people concerned and to those who treat them.

Some professions seem to encourage a tendency to self-destruction. Dentists are most at risk. They are 5.45 more likely to commit suicide than the average. Those in the arts are also in danger. Musicians, actors, dancers, authors, photographers, artists, performers and comedians account for seven out of the thirteen most hazardous professions. Mathematicians and scientists are number eleven on the suicidal jobs list. Unskilled labourers are the least likely to kill themselves. This seems to suggest that intelligence and creativity play a large part in the decision not to be. Could it be that thinking is where it all goes wrong? Thinking inevitably brings tempest on its wings.

With the dawn of intelligence came dark suspicions about the value of life. An ugly day it must have been when the first man came face to face with the idea of the worthlessness and the absurdity of life, when he discovered the grapes were sour, and the apple concealed a worm. On that day a chasm opened at his feet and he was filled with a deep unease that the gods had tricked and deceived him. Nature had a nasty look, always denied his wishes and dashed his hopes. The animals entertained no such doubts. They didn't think and were content to get on with the business of hunting and digestion.

Only man revolts against Mother Nature, against living at all in so preposterous and hostile a world. The Greeks had a story about a Phrygian king who captured the satyr, Silenus, a possessor of supernatural knowledge. The king had only one question: "What is the best, most desirable life for mankind?" Silenus paused for a long moment. "What is best for all," he answered, "is forever beyond your reach. What is best is never to have been born. The second best thing is to die soon." Sentiments echoed by Schopenhauer, the gloomiest of philosophers. The story doesn't record the king's reaction, but Silenus was not heard of again.

In one lifetime the world has changed beyond all recognition. Technology has transformed society and the way we live. Globalization has transformed the way we do business and social media has transformed the way we interact. Perhaps the greatest and most alarming change has largely been ignored by the newscasters, a huge shift to the political left and the rise of hyper-humanitarianism found in the doctrines of political correctness, aka, Woke. They preach sympathy for the weak, and help for the incompetent. Pity, particularly self-pity, is the temper of our times. It is the one virtue that is close to swallowing all the rest. This spread of tender-heartedness has had many unwelcome consequences. It has caused riots, looting and death. It has undermined law enforcement, castrated our politicians, hollowed out our institutions, taken over corporations, deprived ordinary men and women of employment and torn down national heroes from their pedestals in the public parks.

We have come to disapprove of violent sports, anything involving risk. We look on the hunting of hares, foxes and deer with horror. The sight of a butcher's shop nauseates us. If it were possible we'd turn the lion, the tiger, the wolf and our pet cat into vegans. So great is our sensitivity we have to have safe spaces in our universities to protect our delicate feelings from those nasty guest lecturers who might say something unpleasant. Free speech is under threat. Double-speak and delusion is in the air. We seem to be building the kind of society where suicide will flourish.

In 2019 Greenland had the highest suicide rate in the world, while Europe, as a region, was the world leader in self-inflicted deaths. One can understand why the Inuit people of Greenland choose not to be. Greenland is a cold, lonely country, sparsely populated and culturally isolated. A kind of social breakdown which began in the 1970's seems to be at the root of Greenland's problem. Alcoholism, depression, poverty, conflict-ridden relationships with spouses and dysfunctional parental homes. Strangely enough, climate has little effect on the suicide rate. The people of Greenland decide to kill themselves in summer, a cheerful, happy time when the weather is at its best. This holds true for suicides all around the world. June is the favourite month to die.

But why Europe of all places? The citizens of Western Europe are among the freest, most prosperous people in the world. But if the region was to be divided along iron curtain lines, things would look very different in the east where the suicide rate is the highest. Lithuania in Eastern Europe has the highest rate of self-inflicted deaths, and the second highest in the world. Denmark in the west has the lowest. In fact, the lowest suicide rate in the world. What makes these two European countries so different?

On the surface they share many similarities. Both have relatively small populations. Both are developed countries with high incomes and advanced economies. Both rank favourably in terms of civil liberties, press, and internet freedom, and both are members of the European Union. So what is it that makes the people in Demark embrace life, while those in Lithuania yearn for death? How are we to explain the consistently high rate of suicide in one country and the persistently low rate in another? It must be something lurking in the cultural air of these two countries nudging its citizens in one direction or the other.

What categories of people tend to be more susceptible to suicide? Men rather than women, Protestants, rather than Jews or Catholics, the old rather than the young, the newly rich rather than the permanently poor, the intelligent rather than the stupid, the divorced rather than the married, alcoholics rather than the sober, the lonely rather than the affiliated. Clearly, the causes can't be found in individual psychology. Suicide is a social problem, formed by social institutions.

17

THE ROLE OF RITUAL.

EVERY COUNTRY HAS national rituals all their own. Britain has Guy Fawkes Day, America has Thanksgiving and France has Bastille Day. Such rituals help to unify a nation and tell people what to understand about themselves. Society purposely translates its values into rituals that promote social cohesion. These can take the form of national celebrations, family gatherings, sporting events, rock concerts and attending a church service, to the small things like good manners and common courtesies that grease the wheels of commerce and friendship. A person engaged in a ritual is involved in something outside himself. Rituals bond people together for reasons they don't quite understand.

Modern society seems to have forgotten the importance of ritual. The recent pandemic of the Covid virus has panicked governments into choking off this vital source of the élan *vitale*. They have introduced lockdowns that smother social intercourse, separates family members, wrecks the economy and destroys mental health all in the name of saving lives. The government, for the best of intentions, cancels Christmas, closes restaurants and pubs, shuts down sporting events, forbids foreign travel, concerts, theatre performances and public gatherings. All this is done with the best of intentions. And we all know where that leads. Society begins to fall apart when the glue of ritual is absent. Some people decide to die.

PART FIVE

THE UNCERTAINTY OF CERTAINTY

18

THE ORDEAL OF CHANGE

MOST PEOPLE ARE wary of change. They are afraid of it. When faced with something wholly new they shiver a little. Yet for the past three hundred years we've been living through a firestorm of change that is actually gathering force. The men and women of today are on a collision course with tomorrow. The accelerating pace of change is pushing us into the future before we're ready, or able, to adapt. The social impact has been tremendous. It has spawned strange creeds and absurd beliefs. It has brought us a world in which gender has ceased to exist, where people can change their sex by public announcement. Where male criminals calling themselves women are allowed to serve their sentences in female prisons with the expected result – an increase in prison rapes. We've been dragged into a tomorrow where nothing is fixed, everything is in flux, where the language itself is being made muddy and unclear, where reason is under attack and permanence is dead. Small wonder people fear this brave new world change is bringing.

Millions are increasingly disoriented by the feeling of transience and rootlessness. The world they knew is quickly disappearing in the rear-view mirror and the world they are in seems incomprehensible, something they are incompetent to deal with rationally. There are anarchists who, beneath their filthy t-shirts, are outrageous conformers. There are buttoned-down business executives who are outrageous anarchists. There are married priests and Jewish Zen Buddhists. There is malaise, mass neurosis, rampant irrationality, division, free-floating violence, race hatred, anger, opioids and oblivion. Much oblivion.

The term 'culture shock' has been around for a long time. Culture shock is what happens to a traveller when he finds himself in a place where everything means the opposite of what he understands it to mean. A place where yes means no, where fixed means negotiable, where up means down, where the psychological clues that help us to function in society are suddenly with-

THE HEADACHES OF HUMANITY

drawn and replaced by new ones that are strange and incomprehensible.

Think how much worse it would be if this happened to a person in their own country. Or to a whole population at large. The impact would be far more severe than mere culture shock. People would look around with a profound sense of bewilderment at suddenly finding themselves strangers in a strange land. A place where all the signposts have been turned upside-down. Where nothing is familiar. Where there is no hope of retreating to the world of yesterday already half-buried under the onslaught of the new reality. The result would be a severe feeling of dislocation and mass disorientation. The avalanche of change is upon us and most people are grotesquely unprepared to cope with it. This doesn't bode well for social stability.

A nation undergoing drastic change is a nation of misfits. And misfits live and breathe in an atmosphere of febrile discontent. They have lost their footing, their self-esteem and their self-confidence, so in desperation they grab for the next best thing. Substitutes. The substitute for self-esteem is pride. The substitute for self-confidence is faith, and the substitute for alienation is the fusion with others into a united group. It's hardly necessary to point out that reaching for substitutes always spells trouble.

A population undergoing drastic change develops a hunger for faith, pride and unity. It opens itself to all manner of fantastic ideas and irrational beliefs. It is eager to throw itself into collective undertakings designed to hammer the world into the shape of its peculiar ideologies. It generates fanatical attitudes, intolerance, united action and spectacular demonstrations of defiance and civil unrest. To the faithful it feels as if something new and glorious is being born. To the bewildered herd it feels as if something valuable and irreplaceable has died.

19

THE GAME OF CHANCE

CHANCE EVENTS ARE both random and unpredictable. The chance event makes a nonsense of prophesy. There's an old saying that has the ring of truth: God laughs at those who make plans. A chance event can change the course of history, alter the destiny of a nation, or change a person's life in an instant. A chance event can be an accident, a coincidence, a mishap, a misfortune, or a stroke of luck. Whatever form it takes it is always unsuspected, surprising, pleasing, shocking or horrifying.

Science, medicine, business, politicians and professional gamblers hate randomness and chance. They attempt to tame the unpredictable with statistical probabilities. Science uses mathematics, medicine uses diagnostics, politicians use opinion polls, business use risk management and gamblers use odds. What they are searching for is certainty, an elusive chimera that exists nowhere in the universe. Not matter how hard they try something always goes wrong.

On the night of February 18, 1969, Senator Edward Kennedy, the younger brother of John, and Robert, both of whom had been assassinated, was having drinks with friends in an isolated cottage on the tiny island of Chappaquiddick, a three-minute ferry ride from Martha's Vineyard. At the time Senator Kennedy was a shoe-in to win the next presidential election in 1972. He was the golden boy of American politics, the natural successor to JFK. At about 11:30 that night Kennedy left the party with a 29-year-old woman campaign worker called Mary Jo Kopechne. Somehow Kennedy got lost in the dark and sped onto the narrow wooden Dyke Bridge, skidded and plunged over the side into the cold water. Seconds later Edward Kennedy bobbed to the surface and crawled to the safety of the beach, leaving Mary Jo still trapped inside.

Kennedy never reported the accident. Instead he summoned two of his friends and explained what happened. The three of them raced back to the bridge and his two friends plunged into the water while Kennedy broke out in sobs of self-pity. It was dark and the water was cold and the two men failed to rescue Mary Jo, who was probably already dead by this time. Still nobody alerted the authorities. It was not until 8:20 the next morning when the tide receded and the car became visible that a passer-by reported it. The car with the body of Mary Jo inside was soon traced back to Kennedy. When all the details of Kennedy's disgraceful cowardice, his negligence in notifying the authorities, how he'd left a young woman to die to save his own skin came to light, his presidential hopes were over. In a way Mary Jo's death changed the destiny of a nation. Senator Edward Kennedy's craven behaviour and weakness of character in a time of crisis demonstrates the sort of president he would have made. America owes chance and Mary Jo Kopechne a debt of gratitude.

A chance event can affect the entire world. Beavering away in a secret laboratory in Wu Han a group of Chinese scientists were experimenting with gain-a-function viruses, which means they were attempting to make natural viruses more deadly to humans. This research carried out in China was largely funded by American money. If all this isn't strange enough, the virus contrived to escape the laboratory and began to ravage the human population, destroying millions of lives, not to mention the economies of the richest nations. Nobody expected such a terrible thing to happen. Nobody was prepared for it. And, of course, nobody was punished for it. It was an 'oops' moment that cost Donald Trump the presidency, and gave us senile Joe Biden, even more unfit to be president than Edward Kennedy.

Chance events are not always disastrous. The unpredictable weather has played its part in the fate of nations. A chance wind scattered the Spanish armada and saved England from an invasion. The Kamikaze, or the divine wind, saved Japan from a hostile Mongol fleet.

Consider the sudden fog that descended on the East River on August 29, 1776, that allowed George Washington's badly-beaten army to escape to Manhattan. Washington and his exhausted, bedraggled troops were trapped on the high bluffs above the river known as Brooklyn Heights. His back was to the river and the British were closing in with overwhelming force. British warships were sailing up the river to cut off Washington's only escape route. The sudden, fortuitous fog halted the British onslaught and allowed Washington to evacuate his beaten army to the safety of Manhattan, giving him time to regroup and carry the revolution to victory. Without that fog America would never have been born. One can only speculate what the world would be like if the United States failed to exist.

A chance event can change a culture overnight. In the early hours of August 31, 1997, Diana, Princess of Wales, climbed into a chauffeur-driven Mercedes Benz with her playboy boyfriend, Dodi Fayed, the son of a multi-millionaire, for a short ride to an apartment in the Rue Arsèene Houssaye. They never made it. The car was travelling at high speed, trying to outrun the pursuing paparazzi. The driver lost control at the entrance of the Pont de l'Alma tunnel, smashed into the right-hand wall, careened to the left before colliding head-on into the thirteenth pillar supporting the roof. Diana, Dodi, and the driver were fatally injured. Only Diana's bodyguard survived. It was later discovered the driver had been drunk and loaded with drugs. An intoxicated Frenchman had killed the most photographed woman in the world, the mother of two young boys. The consequences of this random death were enormous. The whole world was shocked and horrified. A universal wail of grief rose up for a 36-year-old woman they didn't know. An ocean of flowers flooded the grounds of Kensington Palace. A shrine was erected as if for a saint. The British stiff upper-lip developed a quiver and a drip. It suddenly became rather fashionable to snivel and whine. That night cry-baby culture was born.

The vagaries of chance are built into the very marrow of creation. Those who attempt to control it, let alone understand it, are doomed to fail. Nothing is secure. Nothing is certain. History is made on the spin of a wheel, a roll of the dice, the turn of a card. Every day of our lives is a gamble.

20

DISORDER AND DECAY: THINGS FALL APART

THE PURPOSE OF structure is delay. The stone cracks. The column slips off its pedestal. The tension is released. The weight drops. The roof caves in. Order moves only in one direction, from more to less. That is why time is also a one-way street. Disorder follows time the way one bullet follows another. Neither time nor the bullet is reversible.

The Bible provides some wisdom on the problem of impermanence. Verse 6:19 of the gospel according to St Matthew says: "Lay not up for yourselves treasures upon earth, where the moth and the rust doth corrupt and where thieves break through and steal..." Two thousand years ago it was clear that the disorder of the universe tended towards the maximum.

How disheartening it must have been for early man to discover that everything around him deteriorates. This observation was most likely made on biological objects such as dead animals and rotting fruit. Our ancestors must have seen how the maggots, the worms, the rats and the fungi, the whole process of decay, worked to break down a once living thing to its basic constituents. With the coming of agriculture and settled civilization this observation became a real problem. How to keep food from spoiling was suddenly a vital question. Manufacturing objects of value came into existence. But these were permanent only in a limited way. Blades lost their sharp edges and metals oxidized. The age of rust has been with us ever since.

By the time St Matthew penned his gospel it was well understood that all things were subject to rot and decay. Nothing people treasured had any permanence. Eighteen-hundred years later the industrial revolution was in full swing. The spirit of optimism was in the air. Evolution was moving the world to higher and higher states of perfection. This optimism proved to be an illusion. The industrial revolution held a dark secret. A purely material study of the efficiency of steam engines led to a metaphysics of radical pessimism comparable to the views of the material world held by

Jesus and Buddha. By this strange twist of fate those two old enemies, religion and science, were dancing for the first time to the same tune. *Hi ho, hi ho, it's off the cliff we go.* They both agreed the world was doomed.

The scientific term for disorder is entropy, that is to say the measure of disorder in a system. What prevents things from staying together and remaining in good repair is something called the second law of thermodynamics. This is the law that states that yesterday was better than today. And that tomorrow is going to be even worse. Thermodynamics, prosaically enough, is the study of heat and mechanical work. The first law states that energy can't be created. It can only be converted. It can be changed from one form to another, say from fossil fuels into gasoline. The second law states that in the process of conversion a certain amount of energy is lost. And this energy is unrecoverable. That means that the world and the universe itself is slowly running down like an unwound grandfather clock. All of creation is heading towards a paralysing thermal death. If we live in an expanding universe the spiral nebulae are receding from us at fantastic speeds, 150,000 miles a second. The heavens are changing before our very eyes, but we don't notice it. If man survives until the end of time, a highly doubtful prospect, he will say goodbye to the rest of the universe which will vanish from sight. Entropy will have done its work. The degradation of energy will mean the temperature everywhere will be exactly the same. Nothing will happen. Everything will stop. There will be no energy left to rebuild the burnt-out cosmos. Entropy is the descending staircase to extinction. The universe, unable to keep itself alive, is subject to the same dark destiny as its children. It, too, must die.

21

COUNTER-ENTROPY: THE BIOSPHERE

WHILE THE ENGINEERS of a hundred and fifty years ago were patting themselves on the back for discovering the laws of thermodynamics, biologists were tearing their hair out. They realised that entropy applied only to closed systems that were in equilibrium. If there was one system not closed and not in equilibrium, it was the earth. The earth gets bombarded with solar energy. Although plants absorb only a small amount of that energy, it's still enough to build vast forests and give birth to complex organisms by breaking down the complex bodies of food animals, and digestible fruit and vegetables. The energy that remains is used to copulate and reproduce, build cities, nations and empires. It is also used to make war and destroy what the other guy has built. We also tap the energy of coal and oil to heat our homes, power our factories, light our cities, propel our cars and fuel our planes. The use of fossil fuels has given humanity levels of comfort and prosperity previous undreamed of. Yet, in recent years, the use of such fuels has become an environmental crime, a sin against Mother Nature. The alarmists claim such practices are destroying the planet, accelerating the disorder and increasing the amount of entropy in the climate and the weather system. Ironically, the environmental movement has taken on a dangerous fanaticism that seems to be contributing as much entropy to the social system as carbon dioxide is to the world.

This morning I was sitting at the kitchen table watching my wife do the dishes. It occurred to me just how much effort we put into slowing down the increase of disorder in our immediate surroundings. Housework is a continuous battle against entropy. Our society, until the emergence of women's liberation, had decided that the eternal struggle against disorder was woman's work. Every housewife was doomed to sweeping, dusting, washing the dishes and cleaning the clothes. She was the lowly foot soldier in combat against the second law of thermodynamics. It was a battle that could never be won. There were no victories, no triumphs, or medals for valour. The best one could hope for was a stalemate. Men would build structures destined to collapse. Women were given the thankless task of maintaining these structures against the tendency to crumble and decay.

Entropy always wins in the end. Perfect order requires infinite work. An impossibility. All life depends on solar energy. Here, at the heart of our solar system, entropy is hard at work. The sun is slowing burning itself out. It, too, will die, and with it all life will cease to exist. Darkness and nothingness is our ultimate fate. That is the only certainty in the universe of chance and change and increasing disorder.

PART SIX

Laughter & Tears

22

Laughter: The Accessory Reflex

Laughter is a difficult bacillus to isolate. It serves no biological purpose. Its only function is to provide temporary relief from social stresses and tensions, a discharge mechanism for nervous energy. Why we laugh has puzzled philosophers since antiquity. One might say that evolution gave us laughter to lighten the burden of living in a humourless universe governed by disease, death and the second law of thermodynamics.

There is only a short step from the sublime to the ridiculous. And nothing can be more sublime or more ridiculous than a human being. We don't laugh at a landscape or a city street no matter how charming or ugly. We might laugh at an animal but only because we see something human in its behaviour. Man has been defined as the animal that laughs. He is also the animal that is laughed at. Human beings only find other human beings truly humorous.

Laughter is universal, but what is considered funny is always local, regional, or national. The British accuse the Germans of having no sense of humour simply because they don't understand German humour. The comic effect depends on an acquaintance with local knowledge, customs, manners and social conventions. Laugher is the laughter of a group, a closed circle to outsiders.

In order to be funny humour must contain an element of cruelty. A fat man slips on a banana skin and we laugh at this sudden loss of human dignity. It only ceases to be funny if the man actually hurt himself. Then we'd feel guilty about laughing. That's why we find clowns and clumsy stage comedians funny. When they stumble, trip and fall down nobody gets hurt. We can laugh at them without guilt.

Humour also depends on intelligence. The ability to get the joke. Part of the laugher that a joke provokes involves self-congratulations for being smart enough to understand it. In order to be funny a joke must bring together two incompatible ideas.

Two women meet while out shopping. One

looks happy. The other depressed. The happy one asks: "Why so glum?"

"It's nothing."

"A death in the family?"

"God forbid! If you must know it's my son, Jimmy. His teacher says he must see a psychiatrist."

Pause. "Not serious I hope?"

"The psychiatrist says he's got an Oedipus complex."

"Oedipus shmoedipus," the happy woman laughs. "You have nothing to worry about so long as he's a good boy and loves him momma."

Two incompatible ideas brought together by a misunderstanding. But in order to find it funny you must be familiar with the terms of Freudian psychiatry.

Emotion is the great enemy of comedy. We can't laugh at someone we sympathise with, or identify with, or feel pity for. In order to laugh we must dehumanise the person we're laughing at. The man who slips on the banana skin must be a clown, a performer sent to amuse us. Only then can all our repressed sadism emerge in a burst of savage laughter. In a crowded theatre one burst of laughter will get another until the whole audience is roaring. That is why TV comedy shows use a laugh track to inform the audience when to cut loose. Laughter needs an echo.

Laughter is one form of tame aggression. There

are many others: sports, politics, protesting, bullying on the internet, or writing editorials for the New York Times. Dictators, intellectuals, artists and democratic politicians fear laughter more than the assassin's bullet. The laughter of the people at a bumbling leader, an intellectual who needs to keep his credibility, an artist who wants to be taken seriously, or a politician seeking re-election is always a howl of ridicule, a raucous rejection, a prelude to the tolling of the bell.

There are many kinds of humour. Puns and witticisms, caricature and satire, clowns and impersonators, parody and the practical joke, low comedy and sophisticated humour that appeals to the donnish academic. What these different forms have in common is a drop of acid, a hint of ridicule, a touch of cruelty, overt or disguised, aimed at a person, a group, an institution, a government, or an ideology. Its purpose is to undermine and eat away at the person, the group, or the structure that it opposes. The first group on Hitler's hit list wasn't the Jews. It was nightclub comedians who mocked his speeches and his ridiculous moustache. In the Soviet Union humour disappeared from the public forum and only survived in small, closed, trusted groups. In China today, humour is frowned upon and often punished. Comedy can be a dangerous thing if it is allowed to get out of hand.

Even in the so-called free west comedy is systematically being shut down. Certain types of humour are strictly forbidden. You can't make fun of minority groups, even if the joke has nothing to do with race. You can't make fun of a person's nationality, gender, ethnicity or disability. Gone are the Irish and Polish jokes, the sexist jokes, the stereotype jokes and the stammer jokes. The only legitimate targets available are the white, working-class male, the Christian religion, Jews, and everyone else who disagrees with the progressive left and their insane ideas that go unquestioned by the cowards in charge. Comedians and celebrities and ordinary folks are regularly cancelled for making an inoffensive joke, or a negative remark about a protected person, or group. Public laughter is dying in western culture. The jokes aren't funny anymore. Laughter is no longer a spontaneous outburst of hilarity. It has become a polite gesture of approval for the prevailing ideology. Audiences don't laugh anymore. They titter and inhale an air full of virtue and self-congratulation. The funny guys and gals have been driven from the stage. What's left is shit and it stinks.

The best weapon the intrepid comedian has is satire. This form of humour distorts the characteristic features of an individual or a society by exaggeration and simplification. The highlighted features are those the satirist wants to attack. The deadly tip of satire is irony. Irony has many functions. At its best it is the witty instrument of truth. It mocks, chides, deflates, scorns and exposes. Irony pretends to take seriously what it does not. It purports to support the enemy ideology, applaud its values and its methods in order to reveal their innate absurdity. It praises to the high heavens what it hates. It uses exaggeration to inflate the enemy's ludicrous ideas and policies to such a degree that the only response is laughter. Irony is a subtle weapon. The person who employs it must have the imaginative power of seeing the world through the eyes of his opponent, and the wit to turn that world upside-down.

Beneath the human level there is neither the possibility nor the need for laughter. Such accessory reflex could only arise in a biologically secure species with flexible emotions and intellectual independence. The ability to laugh at ourselves heralds the emergence of self-criticism. It shows a nimbleness of thought which enable it to detach from feeling. Laughter signals the human rebellion against our primitive animal origins, our refusal to remain creatures of habit, to play by nature's rules. The laughter of the first true human being must have been a bark of wonderment and shock. The sound of human laughter entered the world when man perceived the tragic irony at the core of creation. It came with the realization that he'd been tricked.

23

HUMILIATION

HUMILIATION HUDDLES, ALONG with shame and embarrassment, in the shadow of comedy. It's always funny to witness the pompous and the pretentious deflated and humiliated. The virtuous preacher caught with his pants down. The law and order mayor discovered taking a bribe. The married police chief in a hotel room with a hooker and a bag of cocaine. The militant feminist campaigner against pornography who posed for dirty pictures. Humiliation is the punishment that comes of presenting yourself as something you're not. Or believing yourself to be more than you are. It is the balloon of presumption that tempts the pin. Vanity begs for humiliation.

The feeling of humiliation is most keenly felt

by those who fear it most. Some people fear it so acutely they are willing to die rather than look ridiculous. One thinks of Tycho Brahe, the Danish astronomer and bon vivant, whose bladder burst because he was too embarrassed to take a piss. People feel more humiliation farting in a social situation than they do cheating on their income tax, or their spouse. The unzipped fly, the sweat-stains under the arms, the run in the nylons are mere embarrassments. Humiliation is dark. Embarrassment is light. Humiliation is rough justice. Embarrassment is a slap on the wrist.

Dressing inappropriately, or trying to look 'cool' often invites humiliation. The middle-aged man or woman who dresses like a teenager is bound to be sneered and laughed at. So is the bookkeeper who dons the flamboyant clothes of the artist. So is the bodybuilder who puts a sock in his swimming trunks to impress the ladies. Such people are trying to be something they are obviously not. Failure to laugh would be a sin. Just dressing the way you normally do can provoke humiliation. In certain situations the style of clothing may seem pretentious. Think of the bowler-hatted, pin-striped banker stumbling into a working men's bar. He has crossed a boundary into a territory where he doesn't belong. Pretention is not only a vice of the pretentious it is also a function of geography.

Humiliation involves the unmasking of pretension. It is the triumph of reality over appearance. If humiliation has anything to do with comedy, it is black comedy. It is a chance to indulge our malice, the shameful joy of watching the humiliated victim blush and squirm. Our delight in inflicting, or witnessing, a humiliation can never be one of simple amusement. There is a brutality in it, the sheer, sadistic pleasure of kicking someone when they're down. We can excuse our lack of sympathy because the humiliation was deserved. We can even congratulate ourselves for having served the community.

Life is filled with small humiliations. The e-mail that never comes. The dinner invitation that fails to arrive. The unreturned phone calls. The social snubs and the offers of a coffee turned down. Even praise can be humiliating if the object of the praise knows it is undeserved and realises that some of the audience knows it too. Humiliation and shaming often work in concert. The job of shaming is the degradation of status. The job of humiliation is the deflation of pretension. Shaming operates by stripping away the status a person was entitled to before the shaming. Humiliation destroys the illusion that the status was ever merited.

The most frequent form of ritual humiliation is the apology. In giving an apology we are debasing ourselves in front of the person we have wronged. We assume a submissive posture. We confess our faults and our errors. We lower our status and invest the wronged party with a higher status. We display contrition, regret and remorse. An apology is an unconditional surrender. And that is always humiliating.

There have always been rituals of humiliation and shaming. Hazing, dunce caps, scarlet letters, stocks and pillories. In recent years the simple apology has become a central ingredient of public humiliation and ritual shaming. The most innocent remark can provoke the most savage response. Certain subjects are forbidden. Say the wrong thing, offend the wrong group and you'll find yourself under attack. Your reputation will be smeared. Your job will be threatened. Your friendships ruined, your home life undermined by the pressure on the family. You'll wake up in a living nightmare to howls of outrage and demands for a show of remorse. "Apologize! Apologize! Apologize!" But one apology won't be enough. You must go on grovelling and apologizing. When your debasement has been complete you won't be forgiven, or reiterated into the group, even at much lower status. You will have become a despised example, a warning to others who are tempted to speak their mind.

Humiliation not only destroys pretension. It can also be used to destroy free speech.

24

TEARS: THE TRAGIC VIEW OF LIFE

WHY DO PEOPLE shed emotional tears? Why does going to see *Les Miserables* cause us to weep? Charles Darwin thought emotional tears served no purpose. Tears were useful to keep the eyes moist and to wash out irritants. Even today the shedding of emotional tears remains one of the body's confounding mysteries. Most likely, tears are a way of manipulating others. The tears of a baby alert the mother that her infant wants attention. Tears are the favourite weapon of females because they have such a powerful effect on men. Tears and tragedy walk hand in hand in the same way comedy and laughter do.

Tragedy opens the deepest wounds and reveals the cankers inside the human heart. It teaches us about the uncertainty of the world and shows how weak are the foundations upon which we build our lives. It gives us a courageous, open-eyed view of the broken lives all around us, and the pain within us. It reveals the scourged and lacerated face of humanity. There are no fairy tales about heaven, or about eternal bliss. There is no compensation for the suffering of existence. Tragedy offers nothing but darkness, and the void of unfulfilled lives tossed from the womb only to fail.

Greek tragedy didn't care much about the little guy. It was all about the elite, people with titles, wealth and power. Kings and queens and tyrants and heroes who founded cities and created nations. They are tragic figures because they are not ordinary men and women. They possess qualities far above the average. They are noble and virtuous and brave. Their tragedies are brought on not by vice and depravity but by some error of judgement. Goodness, nobility and courage cannot save them from self-destruction, or from the fiendish destruction the fates have in store. Tragedy is the disaster that comes to those who represent, in an exaggerated form, the flaws and the shortcomings of humanity in general. Their destiny has been written. The situation is hopeless. The overwhelming part of tragedy is this absence of hope, of grim inevitability. Tragedy, unlike comedy, demands feeling rather than intelligence.

It wasn't until the 19th century that tragedy noticed that ordinary men and women suffer and fall too. Two Scandinavian dramatists in particular stand out: Ibsen and Strindberg. Their plays were the tragedies of disease, of eccentricity, of bad heredity, of madness and morbid states of mind. They revealed a society that was decadent and rotten, diseased and morally corrupt. Ibsen suffered the most. He was denounced, his plays were cancelled, or booed off the stage. He dissected society in domestic tragedy and what he showed cut too close to the knuckle for comfort. People turned away in horror from the reflection in the mirror he held up.

In the 20th century the grief, the misery and the disasters of ordinary life still held sway. Gradually, the hero and the heroine descended from divine beings superior to all others and above the hazards of the environment, to human beings superior in degree to others and to the environment, to being leaders, superior in degree to others, but not to the environment. Tragedy has continued to fall all the way down to us, ordinary men and women superior neither to others or the environment.

The 21st century seems to reject heroes altogether, their statues are being toppled, they reputations and achievements disparaged and destroyed. The 21st century hero and heroine have become ironic. They are inferior in power and intelligence to us. They are victims, the members of a minority group, disabled, gender fluid, Trans, in any way disenfranchised, or think they are. They snivel and whine at the slights mishap, a stubbed toe, or a broken fingernail. These crybabies demand attention and they get it. They are everywhere, eating away like termites at the very heart of our institutions, in government, in universities and in the media. What they want is absolute conformity to their absurd, utopian ideas. Truth is their first victim and freedom itself is under a sentence of death.

The tragedies of the 21st century are gathering force. Since the beginning of the new century we've had the War on Terror, the climate crisis, the covid epidemic and now the war in the Ukraine. These have been used to terrorise us, silence us and make us comply. A fearful population is a compliant population. The progressive left is using these very same tactics to make us afraid to complain, or even voice a contrary opinion. The west is desperate for leaders, men and women who are superior to us, brave, virtuous, noble, honest and intelligent. We need them to guide us through the coming catastrophes. Instead, we have a bunch of incompetent clowns leading us in a dance macabre over the cliff to disaster and tragedy. Now that really is something to cry about.

25

DISGUST

DISGUST BRINGS FORTH neither laughter nor tears, yet it is intimately connected with both comedy and tragedy. In low comedy toilet jokes are a must. Farts, piss, shit, vomit, semen, snot, foul ordors and bodily orifices are the objects of humour for the very reason that they are normally taboo. It is the violation of norms that allows us to find humour in what is disgusting.

The most popular target of low comedy is the anus. The asshole is the end point of the digestive process. What entered the mouth as food has been transformed into a reeking waste product that threatens contamination. The foul odour of a turd destroys the sublime illusion of status and rank. It's a democratic reminder that everyone's shit stinks. The anus is the essence of lowness. It is made disgusting by faeces, and comical by farts.

Slimy, slithery, oozy, gooey, mucky, sticky, wriggly, oily and viscid are the most disgusting sensations associated with touch. Decaying vegetation and rotting bodies are disgusting to smell and to sight. A hair in the mouth is disgusting to taste. Even hearing does not escape. Certain sounds, screams of agony, the scratching of a rat behind your kitchen wall can arouse both fear and disgust.

Disgust has its own allure. It can attract as well as repel. Sex is a perfect example of this. Consider the human appetite for sodomy. The anus was designed to allow gas and faeces to pass through, yet like the vagina, it can be penetrated. For this reason the anus is also a temptation. It is the gateway to the most personal space of all. Access is the removal of the ultimate limit.

The anus is the source of all gender-bending possibilities. Penetrating a man's anus feminizes him and degrades him. To receive another man's semen is to be humiliated, polluted and defiled. It is to be turned into a woman. Semen is far more revolting to men than it is to females who welcome it as proof of their sexual power. For men, the appearance of semen is a little death and the end of pleasure. Sexual desire always overcomes disgust and usually finds it exciting to do so.

Some rules we don't violate because they are

backed up by strong social prohibitions of the most moral sort. Guilt, shame and our old friend, disgust. Yet we are fascinated by those rebellious souls who break through the barriers: Eve, Satan, Prometheus, Faust and the Marquis de Sade to name but a few. Such gods and criminals populate our myths, our books and our movies. We give them grudging admiration not only for their flaunting the rules that keep the rest of us in order, but for their strong stomachs that seem impervious to disgust. These violators inspire fear, loathing and awe, the same emotions that drive horror, suspense and some religious devotion.

In tragedy the disgust is more profound. It is not the disgust that arises from bodily functions, not something that can be joked about. It is moral disgust. It is the smell of Hitler's gas chambers. The reports of rape and child abuse, of families wiped out in a deliberately-set house fire, of animals being tortured to death, of race hatred, massacres and genocides. The smell of a fresh human turd can make us gag, but not fill us with outrage. Only moral disgust can do that.

Vices such as cruelty, hypocrisy and betrayal invoke disgust. All of these can be found in certain political and social institutions. Prison guards, executioners, the police, lawyers and politicians all have these traits. They are the moral enforcers of society. Without them the social structure would collapse into crime and chaos. The enforcers deal with the moral dirt and some of it rubs off. They are the point where virtue and vice meet, and often collaborate. We are disgusted by the fact that virtue is transient, up for sale and impossible to achieve. The boundaries that separate vice from virtue, good from evil and the pure from the polluted are shockingly porous and poorly guarded. To our disgust, virtue is only too willing to compromise.

Hypocrisy arouses disgust because it stinks of deceit and corruption. It's saying one thing and believing another. Lawyers, politicians and government spokesmen live and breathe in an atmosphere of hypocrisy. So do the fawning yesmen who slime and oil their way into positions of confidence through flattery and kowtowing. The underling's grease works because of the superior's vanity, which make the flattered and the flatterer equally disgusting. One of the real costs of hypocrisy is the distrust, cynicism and paranoia it generates. People start to wonder if such a thing as virtue actually exists. Hypocrisy make us realise that purity is impossible. It demonstrates that the world is what it is, and will get no better.

Wanton cruelty arouses a disgust that can be paralysing in the face of such evil. It makes us feel our own inadequacy. Yet anger, working in concert with disgust, can stimulate outrage against the offender and subject him to the punishment he deserves. The outcome is not always justice. Sometimes it is simply a lynching. Another disgusting practice.

Disgust works well when it is directed at hypocrisy, cruelty and betrayal. But it can also get twisted into stigmatizing people it shouldn't. Disgust takes a moral stance on judgements of beauty and ugliness. The obese, the disabled, the deformed, the mentally ill and the grotesquely ugly can raise feelings of disgust, alarm, contempt, embarrassment, concern, pity or fear. The price we pay for that is guilt. In a less sensitive age we would feel no guilt, only revulsion. Today things are very different. Now, one of our greatest social fears is that we might mock or degrade the underprivileged by accident. That would bring shame. Guilt and shame demands atonement. So we go beyond the call of duty and invite the fattest, ugliest person we know to lunch, publically demonstrating our solidarity and sympathy with the less fortunate. Even doing the decent thing can have a whiff of hypocrisy.

Disgust, along with its close cousins, contempt, shame and humiliation, are the gatekeepers of society's morals. They determine our taboos, the lines we cannot cross. Should disgust lose its power to disgust, the human race would start to reek and wallow in filth.

26

Tragi-Comedy: Celebrities: What Are They For?

Hooray for celebs. How wonderful they are
Hooray for the trivial and the Hollywood star.

FAMOUS PEOPLE GRAB our attention because they are substitutes for the kings and queens and the heroes of Greek tragedy. They stand above us in wealth, status, power and prestige. The performing celebrities entertain us, make us laugh or make us cry. We love them or we'd like to shoot them. They fascinate us. Their personal lives are always of particular interest. When they slip up, or get caught in a scandal or a crime, we are outraged and feel oddly let down by the real person behind the celebrity mask. We feel we have been tricked.

They are not noble, virtuous and brave. They turn out to be just like us. And for that we hate them and cry for blood and long prison sentences when they get caught in wrong-doing. Celebrities are the perfect embodiment of the tragi-comedy played out in real life.

Celebrities don't have to be actors, rock stars, or athletes. A celebrity is anyone who is famous, even without intelligence, beauty, talent or accomplishment. Politicians often fall into this category. So do the British royal family, a fine collection of bumbling nitwits with, perhaps, the exception of the queen. This royal shower of mediocracy stumbles from one scandal to another, decade after decade, and learns absolutely nothing from its mistakes.

Celebrities are there to entertain us, deliberately or not. Celebrities are ubiquitous. Faces impossible to avoid. They have a vast stage on which to parade their virtue. They jump on the bandwagon of every good cause. They add substance and weight to bad ideas and dangerous fads. They also take it upon themselves to lecture and shame us on topics about which they know little. People buy what they sell and believe what they say. A celebrity can turn conventional wisdom inside out.

Celebrities tend to avoid their fans as much as possible. They are far too above the ordinary man or woman in the street to have anything in common. The exalted like to hang out with the exalted. They hobnob with presidents, popes and rock stars. They confer with statesmen and left-leaning intellectuals. They pose with the Delai Lama and other well-meaning do-gooders. They preach for justice and promote conformity. They are bought and paid for by the establishment to support the ideology of the elites. They are puppets whose strings are easily cut. Celebrities live in terror of public shaming and popular disapproval. The drugs and the booze help them to sleep at night.

Trivial celebrities are the most vulnerable, always on the cliff edge of extinction. They have a short shelf-life and will do almost anything to stay in the public eye. So what drives these fame-cravers? Why are they so eager to walk the high wire? They seem to have a deep human need to prove themselves exceptional. They yearn for recognition, renown, popularity, admiration, prestige and esteem. Approval is what they seek. Neglect and contempt is what they most fear.

I can think of two prominent examples of the trivial celebrity. Prince Harry, yet another defective product of the British royal family. This poor guy, arguably the dumbest of a family not noted for their intelligence, has given up everything for love. Because his controlling wife, Megan, didn't like Britain, or the responsibilities of royal life, Harry uxoriously renounced his royal duties, abandoned the royal family and absconded to southern California, the epicentre of the trivial celebrity.

Under the direction of his wife, the balding princeling has done quite well trading on his title and royal status. With Megan doing all this thinking, Harry is desperately trying to expose his bleeding heart to the American people. He's doing his incompetent best to persuade us that being born a royal with prestige, enormous wealth, instant fame, and almost unlimited opportunity is just about the worst thing that can happen to a person. Not only is Harry a victim of his privileged position, he's out for revenge. He's dishing the dirt on his royal relatives. He's spilling the beans. The royals back home are squirming in embarrassment and burning with resentment.

I, for one, am inclined to feel sorry for this pathetic nitwit. His empty head has been filled with Megan's thoughts and ideas. He is no longer the goofy, lovable Harry of old, but a brain-dead zombie mindlessly doing Megan Macbeth's bidding. If this isn't a tragi-comedy I don't know what is. It makes you laugh and cry at the same time. Poor Harry. He has built his new life on a railroad track and the train is coming.

Our second trivial celebrity is the child

prophet, Greta Thunberg. She stands in the media spotlight proclaiming calamity and doom. Not in the distant future, but tomorrow at noon. If we don't change our polluting ways life on earth will perish. We are murdering the planet. This teen crusader is the new Joan of Arc. She leads protest marches that cause massive public disruption. She lectures world leaders with a scowl and a hectoring finger. She's so wise, so dour and serious, a voice we all must listen to. The media love her. But the general public does not. They'd like to burn her at the stake. But there'll be no martyrdom for Greta. The Ukrainian war and the energy crisis has finally shut her up. As she ages into an annoying adult scold, fame will abandon her, leaving behind only a fading echo of a forgotten celebrity. If Christ had lived to be sixty we would have his memoirs, not Christianity.

Mass media make celebrity possible. The media bosses, the shadowy figures at the top of the tower set the schedule, the content and the message. They are the ones with the real prestige and power. They know how to manufacture popular consent. How to crush the critic and squash the dissenting voice. They shape the climate of belief, whip up frenzies and profitable wars. They know how to scare and alarm. The media bosses are the ones to fear. Their power and influence is too dangerous to ignore.

Celebrities have no real power. When they cease to be popular they are casually tossed aside and are quickly forgotten. Celebrities are there as a distraction. To keep our attention focused on their trivial activities while the sinister forces of social entropy go about unnoticed, dismantling our culture brick by brick. Celebrities stand in the spotlight while off stage the lamp of liberty quietly flickers and dies.

Hooray for celebrities. Hooray for their flaws,
Hooray for the nonsense and the Wizard of Oz.

PART SEVEN

Art: The Good, the Bad and the Bogus

27

WHAT IS ART?

SOME YEARS AGO I visited the Guggenheim Art Gallery in Venice. I liked a lot of what I saw, works by Miro, de Chirico, and Max Ernst. All the paintings and sculptures were strange and unsettling. All worth seeing. Then I came across an effort by Jackson Pollock. I stared at for a minute or two trying to figure out what I was looking at. What I was seeing was visual chaos, the very opposite of art. Jackson Pollock had pioneered a new way to create art. He'd take cans of different coloured house paints, dip a stick into them and dribble the paint over the canvas. Sometimes he'd go wild and splash the paint, or spill it from the top of a stepladder. This innovative method demanded no skill, no craftsmanship, no talent, no vision and no inspiration. It had no content, no meaning and no beauty. It had nothing to say and nothing to offer. Anyone could do it. And yet there it was hanging on the wall of a world famous gallery, as ugly as vomit and worth millions. How did this happen? How did such an artless monstrosity become art?

The principal cause was the invention of photography. Before the camera there was no doubt about the painter's aims. They were twofold. The first was to imitate nature as closely as possible. The second was to make the work beautiful. The camera came as a great shock to the artist. It could record nature much more accurately than the artist ever could. It could even produce beauty. All at once the artist seemed to lose his purpose, his reason for being. His job had been usurped by a mechanical devise. He was obsolete.

If the artist was to survive a new kind of art was needed. The camera made realism in painting unnecessary. Meaning and subject matter no longer counted. Subject matter came to be regarded as nothing but bait to attract spectators to the hook. Beauty was merely the sugar coating to make the hook taste better. Such a view is essentially joyless and puritan. It supposes that bait is unnecessary and sugar undesirable. That's why so many contemporary works of art seem inept, fake and ugly, the same works that are consistently praised by a tiny elite of influential critics and art lovers.

This brings us to the second reason for the rise of bogus art. The experts, the art critics and the learned high priests of culture told us the dribbles of Jackson Pollock was art. These men of words spin complicated academic theories about the beauty of non-objective art. They drone on about the lawful organisation of colours, the delightful variation of forms and the rhythm of motifs. They wax lyrical about the latest genius to bring these combinations into perfect harmony to produce yet another phony masterpiece. Not that the art critic actually believes any of this guff. He's essentially a huckster, a public relations man for the art world. His opinion counts. He decides what art is good and what is bad. He creates reputations and markets. He makes art fraud respectable. Strangely, it is the rich elites who are most susceptible to this nonsense. Embracing what the common herd fails to appreciate gives them a sense of superiority, refinement and intellectual gravitas. It enables them to look down on the rest of us with a smirk of contempt. That's why they lap up the bullshit and spend huge sums on fake art that is intrinsically worthless. The ordinary man on the street is more discerning. He knows a piece of crap when he sees it.

The term non-objective art sounds innocuous enough, but it is like the small print in a legal contract that hides the loophole. Calling the murky mess of a Jackson Pollock, or the plain black canvases of Ad Reinhardt, non-objective art emancipates it from the rules of aesthetic judgement. Here non-objectivity and subjectivity are synonymous. Having been freed of all artistic criteria the artist is exempt from any attempt to create beauty, content, interest, relevance, or meaning. Non-objective art detaches itself from the human sphere and enters the realm of the metaphysical where it is beyond interpretation, judgement, or comprehension.

The gurus of gobbledegook often compare abstract art to music. You don't have to understand it. Just *experience it*. They claim it can bring the same joy, relaxation, elevation and animation as a symphony by Mozart. Painting, like music, has nothing to do with the representation of nature, nor the interpretations of intellectual meanings. Whoever is able to experience the beauty of colours and forms has understood non-objective art. But then music too has its absurdities. There is a piano composition by John Cage called 4'33". This consists of the pianist sitting frozen on his piano stool for four minutes and thirty-three seconds of absolute silence. The duration of the silence is 273 seconds. This corresponds to 273 degrees centigrade, or absolute zero where all motion quietly stops. Cage's other compositions are filled with noise: whistles, sirens, car horns, squawks, squeaks, rattles and other annoying sounds that have no harmony or anything else pleasant to the ear. Critics agree that 4'33" is John Cage's finest composition.

There was a time around the beginning of the 20th century that non-objective art was seen as a hoax, or a bad joke. It couldn't be displayed in public without causing howls of outrage, or the sneering laughter of contempt. In the last hundred years things have turned full circle. Time and familiarity has bludgeoned the public into a grudging acceptance of this anti-art. They hold their noses and endure it like a bad smell that can't be avoided. Now, ironically, representational painting, the kind that requires skill and talent, is looked down on and generally ignored by the art establishment.

Fine art seems to have gone off the rails in 1917 when a French charlatan called Marcel Duchamp stuck a urinal on a wall, wittily called it *Fountain,* and declared this was art because *he* said it was art. *Fountain* was the first installation. Since then we've had a Turner prize-winning piece composed of elephant shit, house bricks on the floor, an unmade bed and a rotting banana pinned to a board. The rotting banana I believe sold for $150,000. So, what is art?

Traditionally, art has always been associated with the idea of beauty. Remove the obscuring concept of beauty from art and what is left? Without beauty art becomes another form of human communication. A language of emotion devoid of words. Words were invented to convey thoughts from one person to another. Art was invented to convey feelings. Good art results in the viewer entering into a kind of sympatric communication with the artist. Take beauty away from fine art and what you have left is empathy. Art is a means of bringing people together, of uniting them in the same feelings.

Art is more than just something you hang on a wall, or put on a pedestal. Historically, it is about utility and knowledge. Art is the root of artisan as well as artist. It is also the root of artifice and artificial. The word art covers a great many subjects. The preforming arts. The literary arts, the healing arts, the teaching arts, the industrial arts, the military arts and arts and crafts, which is the production of beautiful and useful things. When a man builds a house or sculptures a statue he transforms matter. He changes its position and its shape. The idea of what he is creating is firmly fixed in his mind. His skill in the manipulation of raw materials will determine the success or the failure of the result. Aristotle defined art as 'capacity to make, involving a true course of reasoning'. So much for Jackson Pollock and his random dribbles, splodges and splashes.

28

WHAT IS BEAUTY?

BEAUTY IS A concept that eludes definition and defies description. Yet we all know beauty when we see it. It is safe to say women think about beauty far more than men. Personal beauty is vitally important to them. Beauty gives them power. As Pascal noted "If Cleopatra's nose had been a little shorter the history of the world would have been very different." Feminine beauty is better than any letter of recommendation. It swings open the doors to wealth and influence. The need for beauty in everyday life becomes apparent when we seek a partner, buy a house, or go on vacation. Everyone wants a beautiful partner, to live in a beautiful home, wear beautiful clothes, be surrounded by beautiful things and spend their vacations in beautiful places. Beauty and money are the best of friends. They stroll through the world hand in hand. The Greeks found beauty in the human form. They brought the nude to near perfection. Christian art found beauty in the suffering and death of Christ. Secular art found it in nature. Modern art often can't find it at all. Yes, some abstract art does possess beauty, but it is an empty beauty. There is no meaning to animate it, nothing to make it more than it is. It looks back at you like a beautiful face lacking a brain. Beauty is more than pretty, but less than the sublime.

Is beauty subjective or objective? This tiresome question pops up in book after book dealing with aesthetics. If you understand beauty to mean the pleasure aroused by a beautiful object, of course it is subjective. Aesthetic is a bendy word that can be applied to any kind of experience that gives immediate pleasure. The warm sun on your skin, a cool breeze on a hot day, looking up at a blue sky, or lying on a golden beach listening to the gentle lapping of the waves, smelling a flower, tasting a peach, scratching an itch or having an orgasm. All these are pleasurable, but they are not art.

Strictly speaking, aesthetics should be restricted to humanly created objects of art: painting, sculpture, poetry, fiction, music, song, dance, opera, the stage-play and the movies. All of these can be called art, but they have no more utility than the pleasure offered by a beautiful day. Their only true function is to please. Beauty can't feed the hungry, heal the sick, prevent crime, or relieve poverty. Yet beauty serves society in ways that often go unnoticed and unappreciated. A safe neighbourhood is a beautiful thing. So is a clean street, a cut lawn and a park full of laughing children. Remove beauty from art and you are left with communication. Remove beauty from the world and joy would soon follow. There would be nothing but Yin and ugliness. The prospect of such an existence is so horrifying it instils the fear of life rather than the fear of death. Beauty is an absolute human necessity.

29

The Naked and the Nude

A DISTINCTION SHOULD be made between the naked and the nude. The word naked implies a body stripped of clothes, huddled and defensive. Nude, on the other hand, carries no uncomfortable overtone. There is no suggestion of coercion. A naked body is a shamed, humiliated body. A nude body is a proud, confident body. Since the Greeks in the 5th century BC until the advent of abstraction in the early 20th, the unclothed human body was the central subject of art.

Art down the ages is full of images of both the naked and the nude. The naked body is depicted as a pathetic, suffering, broken figure. Christ dying on the cross is an example. The nude, on the other hand, is the embodiment of energy, beauty and power. The nude male figure usually comes in the form of Apollo as the athlete, or the hero. The naked male body is portrayed as a defeated, tortured Promethean figure. The female nude is a Venus, an Eve, or an innocent unaware that she is being observed. The illusion of movement is vitally important for the nude. Movement is perhaps the first subject of art. In prehistoric painting it is all about the movement of animals. There are no human figures on the walls of Altamira. Even in later, sophisticated cultures it was still about the muscular bull and the grace and speed of the antelope. Compared to such magnificent beasts the human form seemed awkward, forked, defenceless and feeble, a poor vehicle for the expression of movement.

Once again it was the genius of the Greeks to see the beauty of the human body. They gave it form in their sculptures and paintings. The nude in Greek art was all about the male nude. This bias persisted until the 19th century when the nude came to mean, almost exclusively, the female nude. Perhaps the change came with the realization that the male nude could achieve strength and character, but only the female nude could aspire to beauty. It was Ingres and his theory that beauty consists of smoothness and continuity that replaced nude men with nude women.

A proud, triumphant nude such as Michelangelo's David stands as an affirmation of life. Michelangelo's strenuous genius all but exhausted the heroic possibilities of the male nude. This is in stark contrast to Grunewald's horrifying masterpiece, his altarpiece of the naked, crucified Christ. In this Crucifixion all the sores, the blood, the pus, the contortion of the body, the agony on the face show a living organism in torment. Never before had the suffering of Christ been made so real. Christian art was the art of the naked. Prudishness on the part of the church restricted the naked body to subjects of pathos. The Expulsion, the Flagellation, the Crucifixion, the Entombment and the Pieta, that legendary incident when the dead body of Christ lay across his mother's knees.

The unclothed human body whether it be naked or nude is an expression of all our joys and sorrows. It is there in the ecstasy of the risen Christ. It is there in the contorted faces of the lamenting women. It is there in the triumphant confidence of the athlete and the hero. The nude shows us who we want to be. The naked who we dread to be and the body itself who really are beneath the clothes in which we hide.

30

UGLINESS: A STRANGENESS IN THE PROPORTION

BEAUTY WELCOMES. UGLINESS repulses. In the west we've managed to push ugliness to the unruly margins, sweep it under the carpet and keep it out of sight. Unlike some third world countries where ugliness is on display everywhere, we, the dainty westerners, are caught off guard when we see it. We are surprised and shaken. It arouses feelings of unease, revulsion and guilt. Sometimes fear and dread. We don't want to see it, and will go out of our way to avoid it.

Is ugliness merely something unpleasant to look at? Or is there more to it? Ugliness is closely related to the grotesque, the combining of human, animal and plant forms together in weird and fantastic ways. Ugliness is also linked to horror, to disorder and chaos, to violence and forms of oppression, to abnormality, to distortion, to sexuality and the body, to birth and death, to cynicism and madness, to apocalyptic despair and dystopian visions. Could it be that ugliness serves society in a strange, hidden, left-handed way?

Ugliness in painting has been with us since the Romans. It entered into European art with the excavation of Nero's Golden House in 1480. The designs on the walls and ceilings showed images of monsters fused with animal bodies, bird-like wings, fish tails and human forms blending into leaf-like patterns, weaving together human heads, centaurs, fauns and satyrs. These images were strange and absurd, affecting the viewer with feelings of fascination, amusement, uneasiness and fear. Because they were discovered in the buried halls of the Golden House they were described as works from the caves or grottos, hence the word grotesque.

There seem to be three periods in western art when ugliness came into its own. The 16th century with Brueghel and Bosch, the age of Romanticism with Goya and Gericault, and the 20th century with Bacon and Munch. In all three periods certain animals commonly appear. Snakes, owls, toads, spiders, reptiles, vermin, insects and, above all, bats. There are entangling vines, sinister plants and dark, haunting backgrounds. There are skulls and skeletons, the tools and the technology of torture and destruction, from the rack to the nuclear missile. Ugliness shows us an estranged world where everything is upside-down and the norms and the logic we live by don't work. Ugliness toys with the absurd.

In literature there is no shortage of ugliness. It can be found in abundance in the works of Dante, Shakespeare, Rabelais, Cervantes, Walter Scott, Victor Hugo and Edgar Allan Poe. The 20th century was perhaps the ugliest century since the catastrophic 14th, and that has been reflected by writers like Thomas Mann, Franz Kafka, Gunter Grass, Flannery O'Connor, Eudora Welty and Toni Morrison. All of the above used ugliness to invoke the fallen character of human existence. Ugliness speaks to us about the darker side of human nature.

In the myth of the fall we are said to be rebellious, disobedient creatures reduced from a state of perfection to a state of existential ambiguity and imbued with a propensity for evil. The fallen angel, Lucifer, stands for all of humanity. He was created good, but falls from his goodness becoming distorted and deformed, an ugly caricature of his former self. In this myth evil is presented as a distortion of the good. It is not a separate force in opposition to the good, but a corruption of the good. There was no ugliness in Eden. Ugliness entered the world the moment we did. We brought it with us.

31

SCATOLOGY

IT'S HARD TO think of anything uglier than human shit. It stinks and forces us to look away. Perhaps the most horrifying thing about shit is that we ourselves produce it. It is part of us. It is inside us. Shit is somehow shameful. We defecate in private behind locked doors. To be seen doing it would be a crushing humiliation, particularly if you're a statesman who values dignity, or the queen of England. We do everything possible to deny its existence. We invent polite euphemisms for going to the toilet. We call it 'the little girl's room', or 'the powder room'. No self-respecting woman would announce: "I'm going for a shit." Why all this shame and denial about a perfectly natural function, something we all do? Why is shit considered a swear word, a word we shouldn't use, but, in fact, use all the time to describe almost everything from a TV show, to our wife's cooking, to life itself? The descriptive power of this small, four-letter word is immense. The English language could hardly do without it.

Shit has played a significant, but unacknowledged role in human affairs. The fact that it is ugly and it stinks is responsible for in-door plumbing and air freshener. The fact that it contaminates and causes disease has advanced science and medicine. It has also been used as a weapon of war to pollute the enemy water supply and spread sickness among the troops. It has promoted massive construction projects such as underground sewage systems and vast treatment plants. It has tested the ingenuity of engineers and architects, captured the attention of doctors and lured anthropologists into studying its curious use in ritual and religious ceremonies.

There is much more to shit than meets the eye, or the nose. Its very ugliness and foulness has, ironically, made the world a cleaner, healthier and a less stinky place. The next time you glance guiltily into the toilet give your humble turd a salute of gratitude before you flush.

32

The Sublime

THE SUBLIME IS bigger than beauty. It rises above beauty the way Beethoven rises above birdsong. It reaches to the very limit of human experience in much the same way as a religious epiphany. It brings us as near to God as we can ever get. But it's not the pleasant encounter you'd expect. The sublime arouses fear and trembling, wonder and awe, in the face of something strange and unknowable. It transcends beauty and ugliness, goodness and evil. It's hardly surprising the sublime resides in the house of horror.

A sublime experience is a terrifying experience. It always astonishes and makes all the other emotions freeze into a state of terror. The passions which belong to self-preservation turn on fear, pain and danger. When confronted with the reality of these things there is only pain. But when presented with the *idea* of pain and danger the reaction can be delight. Art and literature are a means of experiencing the sublime without actually coming face to face with it. A roller-coaster ride can produce the same effect in the form of thrills. Should the car leave the tracks the sublime is the last thing you'll experience.

The sublime can move in three dimensions. Upwards towards the divine, sideways to a union with the whole of humanity, or downwards to the demonic powers. The pleasure we experience when someone else is in danger is based on pity. It's even better if the sufferer is a person we dislike. In spite of our pity we take pleasure in witnessing the suffering because we are separated from it by distance. It is not happening to us. Terror is a passion which always produces delight when it does not press too close. Perhaps this need for the sublime originates in the boredom and stagnation of our everyday lives.

For dear old Sigmund Freud all horror was rooted in the fear of castration. It was this sort of speculative generalisation that makes Freud interesting to read, but hard to believe. Surely, there is more to the sublime than a severed penis.

PART EIGHT

Power

33

THE DESIRE FOR POWER

THE DESIRE FOR power like so many other things is a uniquely human trait. Animals are satisfied with very little: food, sex and survival is enough for them. Humans are not satisfied by so meagre an existence because we are dreaming animals. The desire for power is born in the imagination. It is the spur that drives human beings into exertions after their primary needs have been met. Imagined desires are limited only by what the imagination suggests is possible. Such desires are insatiable and infinite. Perhaps that's why lasting happiness eludes us. Earthly powers are limited by other earthly powers. Earthly power, itself, is terminated by death. Everybody wants to be the boss, but only a few, the distant cousins of Milton's Satan, dream of being God and refuse to admit the limitations of human power. So, what is power and why do we crave it? Power can be defined as the production of intended outcomes. Or more simply by the ability to impose our will on others even if they resist it.

A distinction should be made between traditional power and newly-acquired power. Traditional power is supported by habit and established customs. It is the system we know. It does not have to justify itself, or prove its case in the court of public opinion. Because traditional power feels secure it is usually tolerant and doesn't organise witch-hunts, or pogroms, or send agents among the people to sniff out traitors. Traditional power tends to be benign. It can rely on public opinion to a greater degree than newly-acquired power.

Power is to society what energy is to physics. Like energy power has many forms and is always passing from one form to another. Wealth, military might, political authority and influence over public opinion never operate independently. No one can be truly powerful unless they have control over the major institutions that govern their society. Leading politicians and key government officials command these institutions. So do admirals and generals. So do financiers, the owners of huge business enterprises and the CEO's of the larger corporations. Only within and through such organisations can power be held and sustained.

The most artful democratic politicians are those who succeed in abolishing democracy and setting themselves up at dictators. The covid pandemic gave Justin Trudeau, the notoriously woke Canadian Prime Minister, the opportunity to show the totalitarianism that lurks in the heart of every left-wing progressive. This temptation to exert dictatorial powers over a terrified populace was as catchy as covid. The democrat prime ministers of Australia and New Zealand also fell victim to the virus of power. It should be remembered that Lenin, Mussolini and Hitler owed their success to democracy.

Power can be inherited as in a monarchy, or a tyranny. Hereditary power has given us the idea of the gentleman and the blue-blooded aristocrat. Many tyrants begin life as friends of liberty. One thinks of the affable country physician, Papa-Doc Duvalier, dictator of Haiti and patron of the terrifying Ton-Ton Macoutes. Papa-Doc's son, Baby-Doc, inherited Haiti from his father in 1971 and managed to bleed his desperately poor country dry for the next fifteen years until he was overthrown in 1986. Democracy was invented to stop this sort of thing.

Power can also be acquired by war, revolution, a coup, assassination, or by more peaceful means such as an ability to lead, or votes in the ballot box. In a democracy where there are no limiting factors such as aristocracy or a monarchy to impede the number of candidates seeking power, those who desire it the most are the most likely to get it. Although the love of power is among the strongest of human incentives it is not distributed evenly. It can easily be derailed by the love of pleasure, comfort, ease and approval. Those who lack the will to power can never change the course of events. The power to change the course of history for good or ill belongs exclusively to the powerful. The rest of us are merely spectators in the unfolding drama.

34

Leaders and Followers

WHEN PEOPLE MARCH to the leaders' tune they do so out of self-interest. They seek to acquire power through the group the leader commands. People submit to a leader only when they believe themselves incompetent to command. Whenever there is danger they flock to someone who can take charge. Some of the strongest leaders in history have been thrown up by war, or revolution. Napoleon, Lenin, Mussolini and Hitler are four examples of leaders who came to power as a result of vast social upheavals. Lenin and Hitler fall into one category of leader. Napoleon and Mussolini into another.

Lenin and Hitler were men who believed they were the saviours of their nation, men with a political philosophy and a cosmic purpose. They cared little for the rewards of power. Luxury and ease held no interest for them. They were Spartans. Both of them were men of faith, conviction and courage, coupled with the superior ability to inspire their followers with enthusiasm and zeal.

Napoleon and Mussolini were primarily driven by self-interest. They were soldiers of fortune. They loved power for the rewards it would bring. The revolutionary armies Napoleon led thought of themselves as liberators of Europe. Napoleon, the first modern tyrant, thought no such thing. He limited the amount of liberation to what was useful to his own political position. Mussolini, the weakest of the four, made the trains run on time, but he failed to transform the pleasure-loving Italians into the fierce Roman legions of old. Both of these men were buccaneers who used organised greed with little disguise to gratify their own aims and personal grandiosity.

To acquire the position of leader the candidate must excel in the qualities that confer authority. Self-confidence, decisive action, iron will, quick decision-making, skill at instilling belief in his followers and inspiring both fear and admiration in his allies as well as his enemies. The drive for power is limited only by timidity. Timid souls who are easily frightened shy away from power and gratefully submit to a leader who offers protection and security. This sort of timidity is reduced by the habit of responsibility. Having responsibilities tends to increase the desire for power. Power enables us to realise desires that wouldn't be possible without it. In addition it secures deference from others, thus enhancing self-esteem. Once in command the leader is now in a position to inflict cruelties, rather than to suffer them.

The tyrants of the 20th century often resemble the emperors of Rome. Compare a musical concert given by Nero to a public speech given by Stalin. No one was allowed to leave the theatre while Nero warbled and plucked his lyre. The gates were barred and women were forced to give birth in silence while the emperor sang. Some men were so bored by the music and the applause they faked death and were carried away for burial. When Stalin finished speaking all his hearers were terrified to be the first one to stop clapping. Everyone looked around despairingly and went on clapping, sweat beading their foreheads, fear fighting exhaustion.

For the timid, submission to a leader provides the security of an organization and the reassurance of belonging to a group who all feel alike. Collective excitement is wonderfully intoxicating, but socially dangerous. In the grip of such excitement reason is easily lost along with our humanity, opening the door to massacres and willing martyrdoms.

A skilful orator, such as Hitler, can stir up war-like emotions, producing in his audience two layers of belief. In the top layer the power of the enemy is magnified so great courage is needed to defeat the impending threat. The under layer is a firm promise of victory. The two layers combined inspire heroic feelings and faith in the ultimate triumph of good over evil. This can lead to riots, insurrections and to war. The ideal audience for this type of leader is one given over to emotion rather than reflection. An audience full of fear and hatred, impatient of slow and prudent methods, is a potential mob primed to plunge into madness and murder.

Once men sold their souls to the Devil in return for magical powers. Nowadays, magical powers are conferred by science. And some of the world's leaders have become devils with the ultimate power of destroying life on earth.

35

THE POWER OF OPINION.

THE ULTIMATE SOURCE of power is the control of opinion. Control what the people think, manufacture belief, magnify an enemy threat, inspire fear in the population and all the other powers, military, economic, legal and political will fall into line. The first step in manufacturing belief must be taken by persuasion alone. Once a minority has been converted, then force can be exerted to insure the right message is foisted on the rest of the community. Once the majority have been turned into true believers, the use of force becomes unnecessary.

To produce a mass belief of social importance three factors are essential: desire, evidence and repetition. Without desire or evidence there will be no belief. Of the two, desire is the most important. Where the evidence is skimpy, or nil, more propaganda and repetition is needed to manufacture belief. Repetition is the key to influencing public opinion. Say something often enough and people come to believe it. Teach it in schools, broadcast on radio and television, report it in the newspapers, show it in the cinema, spread it over the internet while, at the same time, smothering dissenting opinions are the seven league boots to power.

Propaganda is only successful when it is in harmony with the mood of the public. A population must desire something: social welfare, stronger, or weaker, police, a higher standard of living, better health care, an end to injustice, or the greatness of the nation. In the absence of collective desire the message of the ruling elite is viewed with a smirk of cynical scepticism. From the governmental point of view democracy enjoys an advantage. It makes the average citizen easier to fool because he believes the government is *his* government.

Organized propaganda on a large scale is practised by commercial advertisers, political parties, the elites and the state. All of these forces usually work together to promote their agenda, or to maintain the status quo. The rise of the tech giants, Google, You Tube, Facebook, Twitter and the others, broke the stranglehold of the mainstream media. They gave a platform to the voiceless and the ignored. This seemed to add meaning to the word 'democracy'. Then, during the presidency of Donald Trump, all that changed. Democracy was getting out of hand. The people had too much say, and what they were saying the tech giants didn't like. The tech giants realised they could act as public censors, screen and decide what information was suitable for public consumption. People with dissenting views were suddenly cancelled, kicked off the platform and banished to oblivion. The naked power of the tech giants was shockingly revealed when Twitter banished Donald Trump, the sitting president of the United States. Who gave Twitter the right to do such a thing? Who elected Twitter to spare us the thoughts of a sitting president? Who made Twitter the gatekeepers of information? The authority of the tech giants doesn't come from government, or any civic institution, nor does it come from the public at large. The tech giants have elected themselves the guardians of 'right think'. They've transformed themselves from nerdy awkward geeks into a sinister thought police, a kind of Gestapo of the mind. In the case of Twitter, change is in the wind. The richest man in the world, Elon Musk, has just bought the company. Elon claims to be a champion of free speech. We shall see.

War is the wild card that changes the game. A

bad defeat destroys belief and arouses rage and a lust for revenge. It shows the government to be dishonest and impotent, ripe for a violent overthrow. That's why after every major war there is always a rich crop of revolutions.

The part played by propaganda in national power has increased with the development of communication technology. A nation can't be united or secure without a unifying belief. A nation can't wage war or defend itself unless people are willing to suffer hardship and to die for the cause. Propaganda is necessary to motivate people to extremes of self-sacrifice. In order to produce such willingness the people must be persuaded that the conflict is about something important, so important that it is worth killing and dying for. Propaganda played a huge part in the allied victories of the First and the Second World Wars. It was also responsible for the American humiliation in Vietnam.

It is easy to overestimate the power of official propaganda if it insists on dishing out false propositions which in time will be seen as ridiculous. When all opposing propaganda is forbidden, rulers come to think they can make people believe anything no matter how outlandish. In time they become overweening and careless, too flagrantly indifferent to the interests of the general population. The indifference of popes gave us Luther and the Reformation. The indifference of industrial

Capitalism gave us Lenin and Communism. Lies need competition if they are to retain their vigour. Without a strong opposition some new Lenin, or a Napoleon, will eventually appear to expose the lies and challenge the authority of the state.

36

Naked Power

War and conquest are the most obvious forms of naked power. A defeated nation has no choice but to submit. In time naked power relaxes its grip and turns into traditional power. All the conquered provinces of the Romans soon became loyal subjects of the empire. The exception were the Jews. The Welsh caved in to the English, but the Irish did not. Military conquest is never stable unless it wins the hearts and minds of the conquered nation. Power is naked when it is respected for no other reason. Governments use naked power in relation to some of its subjects, but not to others. Criminals and traitors are subject to naked power. Law-abiding citizens are exempt.

Most of the great atrocities in human history

have been the result of naked power. War is only one such horror. The slave trade, the exportation of conquered peoples, the inhumanity of early industrialism, the cruelty to children, judicial torture, concentration camps, religious persecution and the treatment of the Jews are a few examples of naked power applied to defenceless victims. A certain amount of naked power is necessary when it comes to rebels or criminals. However, if life is to be tolerable there must be as little naked power as possible. Otherwise, existence would be a grinding misery relieved by moments of acute terror.

37

Revolutionary Power

Revolution is only possible when the prevailing authority has been discredited. The blunders and abuses of government are never quite enough to bring it down. It takes an articulate minority to light the fuse. Every revolution begins with disaffected intellectuals, the men and women of words who want change. Intellectuals with a grievance undermine institutions, discredits those in power, weakens loyalties, mocks current beliefs and paves the road to revolution.

Society depends on deep-seated feelings of love and loyalty, beginning with the family and the neighbourhood and spreading out to the country and the culture as a whole. At the foundation of society is the need every citizen feels to be part of something larger and more enduring than the ephemeral self. Communities are held together not by self-interest, but by a sense of membership and duty, by the feeling that one has a place in the community, even if it's a lowly place. These are the things the disaffected intellectual chooses to attack. To destroy the foundations of a culture is to invite a new, usually Utopian, culture to take its place.

The superior individuals, politicians, intellectuals, writers, artists, financiers, scientists and the corporate elite play a large part in shaping the culture of a nation. They tend to ignore the other great force that can shape a nation, its least worthy members: the deplorables, the failures, the misfits, the outcasts and the criminals, the people who lost their footing in society, or were never allowed to join the ranks of respectable citizens. The discarded and the rejected at the bottom of the heap are important because they possess a latent power. They have nothing to lose. They are always ready to wreck and tear everything down. All they need is a strong leader to unite them and to point to a better future. Those at the bottom are among the earliest recruits of a revolutionary movement.

Once the disgruntled intellectuals have done their work they are quickly pushed aside by the fanatic whose natural environment is chaos. When the old order begins to crack, the fanatic storms in to indiscriminately destroy everything he can. He delights in the sight of ruins and glories in the world coming to an end. Revolutions seldom succeed without the fanatic. Had there been no Lenin the Soviet Union would not have existed. Without Hitler there would have been no Nazi party and consequently no holocaust and no Second World War. The problem with fanatics is that they always go too far. They can't settle down to the business of consolidation. Instead, they breed dissension in the ranks. With no more outside enemies to destroy the fanatics make enemies of each other. Either that or they drive the movement to achieve the impossible. If allowed to have his way the fanatic will eventually destroy himself and the movement he leads.

To consolidate the achievements of the revolution a practical man of action is needed. Only he can save the revolution from the suicidal recklessness of the fanatic. If Hitler had died in the mid-thirties, Goring would probably have taken over and the Nazi movement would have survived. If Trotsky had won the power struggle with Stalin the Soviet Union would have been a very different place, not a better place, just a different place. Stalin's horrible blunders, the extermination of the Kulaks, the paranoid purges, the murderous five-year plans, the gulags, the persecutions and the show trials would never have happened. Without the man of action revolutionary power will degenerate into naked power.

38

Economic Power

Economic power cannot stand alone. It needs force, or the threat of force to back it up. The economic power of private individuals depends upon the law. The economic power of the state depends on the military. Every state runs a sort of protection racket called income tax. Here the reign of force is disguised as the rule of law. Economic power is ultimately derived from the law and public opinion. Yet it can operate independently, usually with stealth. It can influence the law by means of bribes and control public opinion with propaganda. It can put politicians under obligation which interfere with their freedom. It can even threaten to cause a financial crisis. But there are limits to what it can achieve. Where public opinion is strong and firmly decided on an issue, propaganda is useless. Only if the public is undecided or confused can propaganda bring about the desired result. In those places where the law is weak the money-lenders are always in danger. Revolutions and times of social upheaval are particularly hazardous. Before leaving for the Crusades the crusaders made a practice of murdering their Jewish bankers and burning the books to remove the evidence of indebtedness. This is a common theme often repeated throughout history.

In every developed country economic power belongs to a small elite. The possession of economic power can lead to military power as well as the control of propaganda through the media. Today, the most important form of economic power is the ownership of raw materials and the production of food. A modern country can't run without oil to heat homes and fuel vehicles. Nor can it wage war, or protect itself from an invader. The same with food. National survival depends on the control of large areas of fertile land.

The so-called global warming crisis has changed everything. Countries once self-sufficient in raw materials have virtuously stopped exploiting their natural resources to save the planet. Now they import their oil, gas and coal from other, less fastidious, nations such as Russia, Iran and

Saudi Arabia. Relinquishing the energy supply of a country to a foreign power is like handing a loaded gun to a greedy rival. How can the leaders of the western democracies be so foolish, incompetent and short-sighted?

With the Russian invasion of Ukraine the chickens have come home to roost. The western leaders are beginning to realize that globalization may not be such a good idea. The search for cheap labour has moved jobs from the rich countries to the poor. The CEO's of the multi-national corporations don't worry about the exploitation of the poor abroad, or the misery of the unemployed back home. Nor do they worry about the civil unrest, the protests and riots that shipping jobs overseas can cause. Some nations are better at taking than making.

Once Spain was the richest country in the world. It accumulated enormous wealth through the military conquest of Mexico. Inca gold and silver bullion flowed into the Spanish treasury. This windfall money proved to be a disaster. The Spanish stopped manufacturing its own products because it could afford to buy everything it needed from other countries. It squandered its new-found wealth in exotic luxuries, pleasure seeking and enervating indolence, but mostly in war, that most expensive of pastimes. The money went to pay for soldiers, weapons and provisions that were lost on the battlefields of Italy and Flanders. The Spanish had no qualms about trading with their enemies. Iron cannon from the English. Ships from the Dutch and horses from the Flemish. Spain thought the whole world was working for it. How wrong they were. The flow of Inca gold and silver eventually dried up and Spain went into a long decline. Spain became poor because it had too much money for its own good. There is a lesson here for the United States.

The victory of the allies in the Second World War made America great. It stayed great because of military power and economic skulduggery. Should oil or any other vital resource be discovered in a poor foreign country, America will send in a smiling, clean-cut graduate of an elite business school to tempt the president with visions of a fabulous future for him and prosperity to his poverty-stricken nation. The president is dazzled by the prospect of electric power systems, dams, highways, ports, airports, shopping malls, industrial parks, lavish hotels and the idea of tourism. The clean-cut American might offer to rent equipment from the president's brother at twice the going rate so the brother can kick-back a share of the profits. He could make similar deals with the president's friends in relation to Coca Cola bottling plants and other lucrative business enterprises. All the president had to do was sign off on a world bank loan that would hire US corporations to build the new infrastructure. Most of this loan money never leaves the United States. It is simply transferred from the banking offices in Washington to the engineering offices in New York, Houston and San Francisco.

The elites of the poor country prospered. Everyone else suffered. Money that had been budgeted for health care, education and other public services was diverted to pay the interest on the loan. The loan itself could never be paid. The country was shackled with permanent debt. Then the men from the International Monetary Fund would show up and demand the country sell its natural resources to the United States at cut-rate prices. The country is forced to privatise its electric, water, sewers and other public sector institutions and sell them off to American corporations. They also make sure that the debtor country buy airplanes, weapons, farm equipment, computer technologies and other goods and services from the good old US of A. For decades Uncle Sam called the shots.

Those leaders who fail to cooperate are either overthrown, or assassinated. Their planes blow up, their limos blow up. They are poisoned, shot, or suddenly drop dead from mysterious causes. There is a long list of such leaders, names like Mossedegh of Iran, Arbenz of Guatemala, Allende of Chile, Lumumba of the Congo, Diem of Vietnam, Noriega of Panama and Saddam Hussain of Iraq. The CIA jackals know how to deal with obstinate leaders who put their country first, or who become political embarrassments. That's what the clean-cut American doesn't tell the president before he signs off on the World Bank loan.

Now American economic supremacy is being successfully challenged by a determined rival – China. China's success is due to its friendly softly, softly approach. Third-world countries prefer to deal with China because China, unlike the US, doesn't kill or overthrow their leaders. Small, poor countries fear America. They fear the Pentagon, the CIA, the NSA, the drones, the missiles and the bombs. China is capitalizing on the fear generated by the United States. A system based on fear can work effectively in the short term, but it never lasts. That is a lesson America is only just beginning to learn.

It didn't take long for the people in the poor nations to see that they were being exploited. But, until China stepped into the ring, they had no place to turn except the United States. There was no counter-balancing power. China has learned from the mistakes of the United States. It doesn't attach draconian demands to its loans. There are no harsh World Bank, or International Monetary Fund conditions such as voting the right way on UN resolutions, or trading only in dollars, or allowing military bases occupied by foreign troops. China doesn't arbitrarily pull the economic plug and move their corporations to another more economically attractive country. Instead, they promise the factories they build will continue to operate in the long-term. China has reformed and refined the American model, but the aim is just the same – to control countries and exploit their resources. The world order is changing in favour of Beijing while America continues to slip further and further behind.

PART NINE

Uncle Scrooge

39

THE SECRET LIFE OF MONEY

How many of you can name the 25 richest people in the world? It's a fluid list, always changing. Some of these people are celebrities. At the moment, Jeff Bezos has been bumped into the number two spot by the new king of the hill, Elon Musk. Bill Gates is number four and Mark Zuckerberg has slipped to number twelve. Others are virtually unknown. Sixteen of the 25 are American, including two women. Alice Walton, who inherited 55 billion from her daddy, the founder of Walmart, making her the richest woman in the world. And Mackenzie Bezos, the ex-wife of Jeff, founder of Amazon and the second richest man on the planet. Not all of the people on the rich list have the Midas touch, but their daddies, or their ex-husbands, do.

A billion is a thousand million. That's a one followed by nine zeros. The richest man ever, Elon Musk, is worth in excess of two hundred and fifty-six billion and climbing fast. That's more than the entire GDP of some poor countries. More than the cost of the pandemic to the British economy. It is a shocking, almost incomprehensible, amount of money for one man to possess.

Throughout history vast amounts of money have induced some bizarre and richly perverse behaviour. Today, men and women possessed of great wealth are crowned with the qualities of infallibility and awe that once belonged to popes and kings. They are imagined to be the smartest people in the room, geniuses who can see in the dark. The ones who've mastered the occult secrets of high finance. They are showered with honours, awards and appointments to important positions. They serve as advisors to presidents and prime ministers. They become expert commentators on subjects they know very little about. Their advice on every subject is eagerly sought. They have great influence. No wonder their heads swell up like over-heated investment bubbles. No wonder they are filled with hallucinations of their own divinity like mad Roman emperors such as

Caligula and Nero. They think wealth and power sets them apart from the rest of us, which it does. They think they are above the law, which they are. They even come to believe that they are immune from death, which they are not.

Money confers much more than power, privilege and awe. It also confers something magical called prestige. Those familiar with the origins of the word 'prestige' smirk disdainfully at its use. They know that it is associated with trickery and sleight of hand. The prestige is the third and most difficult part of a magic trick, the payoff that stuns the audience with misdirection, skill and cleverness. There's something sly and fraudulent about prestige. Perhaps that's why it's bestowed so abundantly on the super-rich. Knowledgeable people prefer honour. Honour is a cleaner word without a murky past or a questionable reputation.

Only those at the very top possess the magic of prestige. Power, status, royal birth, money, awards and civic honours are the basis of prestige. Without at least one or two of these advantages the magic is likely to pass you by.

People with prestige are looked up to and admired. They float above us in another sphere like the old, flawed gods of Olympus. The only thing that separates them from us is money. They seem so smug, secure, confident and untouchable. They make us jealous and angry. How we love to watch these smug, rich bastards fall. The shameful joy we feel when they tumble in disgrace from the sky, undone by hubris, folly, or criminal acts. We feel justice has somehow been served when they lose their money, their prestige and the awe and admiration that goes along with it. Without their money they are gods no longer. Just raggedy-ass mortals like the rest of us.

So exactly what is this stuff we call money? Money is primarily a medium of exchange, something that buys goods and services and used to settle debts. It was invented in Lydia around the 8th century BC when some bright spark hit upon the genius idea of using bits of metal as a medium of trade. This was the birth of coinage, an earth-shaking eureka moment in human history. It was also the birth of financial skulduggery, counterfeiting and white collar crime. Hard-pressed rulers quickly hit on the notion of secretly reducing the content of precious metal in their coins. A smaller amount of gold and silver would buy as much as before. Businessmen were just as sneaky. Before making a deal they would clip or shave a bit off the coin giving them a tad more profit in the transaction. The result of all this was Gresham's Law; bad money always drives out good. That is to say people would sensibly hoard the good coins and circulate the bad. This is the only economic law in history that has never been challenged.

With all these clipped, filed, sweated, trimmed and adulterated coins in circulation something had to be done. So banks were invented to deal with the problem. The first notable public bank was established in 1609 in Amsterdam, a major financial centre at the time. This was the next great step in the secret life of money. The solution was weighing. The bank took the bad coins out of circulation. Harsh penalties made clipping and debasement of the currency not worth the effort. As always in the secret life of money every solution to a monetary problem leads to new, and usually greater, abuses.

For a hundred years the Bank of Amsterdam functioned usefully and honestly, holding the money of its clients in the vaults and not loaning it out. In 1672 the armies of Louis XIV marched on Amsterdam causing a panic. Merchants besieged the bank demanding their money. When they discovered the money was actually there and that they could be paid they no longer wanted to be paid. This is one of the strange paradoxes of money and banking. In times of panic if people can get their money they no longer want it.

The bank survived because it had enough hard coin to pay out all its depositors. But a new and decisive step was about to be taken that changed all of that. The Bank of Amsterdam began using its depositors' money to make loans to the East

India Company. When the company failed it took the bank with it and left the lives of its depositors in ruins. This basic scenario has been repeated over and over again down the centuries and persists to this very day. The more things change the more they stay the same.

There are three primary sources of money: mints, treasuries and banks. The way banks create money is surprisingly simple. So simple it's almost disappointing. Something as important as money creation should be an arcane and mysterious process like alchemy or the practice of black magic. But all it really takes to create money is the stroke of a pen.

The wily bankers quickly discovered they could use their depositors' money to make loans. The depositor was already on the books as a creditor. The loan created a new deposit. Both deposits could be used to make payments, both could be used as money. Creating money was that easy. I wish someone had told me about banking sixty years ago when I was young.

The secret life of money runs through human history like the Nile through Egypt producing cycles of famine and plenty. It finances wars, sponsors vast inequalities and untold human misery. It also contributes much to the betterment of humankind. It builds hospitals and research facilities, develops new medicines and vaccines to combat and cure disease. It builds the houses we live in, roads we travel and the cars we drive. It fills the world with luxuries many can't afford. It creates conflict, envy, hatred and greed. All too often it brings out the very worst in us. And yet money is not the root of all evil. Money is simply a convenience. Human avarice, the Uncle Scrooge that lives inside us all, is the real culprit.

40

Is Global Capitalism a Giant Ponzi scheme?

A PONZI SCHEME is a form of financial fraud. It is a phony investment company that lures suckers in with promises of high returns on their money. But no investments are made. The fraudster pays his clients from the money he gets from new investors. Growth is essential to a Ponzi scheme just as it is to global capitalism. But the similarities don't end there.

Banks, the heart of global capitalism, do the very same thing as a Ponzi scheme. They take money from one person and give it to others in the form of loans. If something bad should happen and the borrowers can't pay back their loans, the bank will crash. Just as a Ponzi scheme will crash without new investors.

In the United States the social security system works the same way. Today's working generation are paying for the generation that came before them. If the next generation fails to provide enough workers there won't be enough money to pay the current generation and the system will crash. Banks, social security systems and Ponzi schemes all put their faith in perpetual growth. Faith is a poor substitute for certainty. Perpetual growth smells kind of fishy to me, like the dream of perpetual motion.

Money-making is a talent, something akin to the ability to paint like Leonardo, write like Tolstoy, box like Ali, sing like Sinatra, or tap-dance like Bill Robinson. It's in the genes. It's a hunger to excel, to be the top dog, to demonstrate superiority and show the world you're different from everybody else.

Of all the talents nature bestows, money-making is the lowest and most disreputable. There's something unholy about being super-rich, something suspicious and perhaps illegal. As Balzac wrote: "Behind every great fortune lies a great crime". All the major religions despise wealth. The poor of the world seethe with jealousy and rage at the inequality money brings. The middle class squirm and scheme to get more of it. And the rich live like the barons of the Middle Ages in vast estates. They build fortified castles protected by private guards. They live behind high walls in gated communities, shut up in ghettos made for millionaires. I wonder if they shiver in fear in those rare moments when they glimpse the poverty and boiling discontent that surrounds them. They know how vulnerable they are. They know that envy is a weed that should never be watered. For that reason many of the super-rich shun the limelight the way vampires do the sun.

In the United States, the epicentre of the 2008 financial crash, only one person was sent to jail, a Credit Suisse trader with the suspiciously un-American name of Kareem Serageldin. All the others, the bankers, the CEO's and the asset managers walked away unscathed from the devastation they created. They hardly gave a thought to the suicides, the personal disasters, the business failures, the fractured families, the ruined charities and all the rest. They walked away scot-free to the pop of champagne corks and the reward of huge bonuses for destroying so many lives, not to mention the world economy. Well done, chaps. You got away with it... again.

The poster boy of the 2008 collapse had nothing to do with the crash. Instead, he was a victim of it like so many thousands of others. His name is Bernie Madoff and the crash exposed him as one of the biggest financial criminals of all time. Bernie was running a huge Ponzi scheme that clipped his friends, relatives and clients to the tune of 65 billion. Thousands were ruined. More suicides and shattered lives, including his own. Bernie lost everything. His money, his family, his reputation and his freedom. Kareem Serageldin got off lightly. He was sentenced to two and a half years for his part in the financial melt-down. Bernie Madoff, who had nothing to do with the crash, got a whopping 150 years. Poor Bernie. He didn't stand a chance. He was a minnow swimming in a sea of sharks.

A Ponzi scheme, like global capitalism itself, is built on confidence. A loss of confidence in the currency can spell disaster for a nation. A loss of confidence in the stocks and shares of a company can bring that company down. The world economy depends on confidence every bit as much as it does on money, investment and power. Bernie Madoff got away with his Ponzi scheme for more than twenty years because people had confidence in him, the confidence that he was an investment wizard with the Midas touch. It was all a lie, a huge fraud. Bernie was just another adroit conman good at cooking the books.

It's not always the super-rich that have the most power. The real power lies with the bankers, asset managers and the CEO's of transnational corporations, the big money players who manage the dosh for their billionaire investors. Seventeen top asset management firms and banks control a staggering total of 41.2 trillion dollars. This is more than 16% of the world's total wealth. This huge sum is in the hands of 199 key managers. These 199 men and women are the ones who actually run the world.

Growth is the obsession of every banker, asset manager and CEO. Their job is to make money for their investors, to keep the money growing at a rate of three to ten percent. Zero growth spells disaster. The roof timbers begin to crack quickly followed by the collapse of the whole structure.

But there is a problem. With so much cash sloshing around the financiers are running out of things to invest in. So they invest in each other. The seventeen core financial companies all own large chunks of stock in each other. Their executives sit on each other's boards. They work together to rig the whole financial system in their favour. With the help of tame politicians they wangle tax breaks, subsidies, bailouts and government deregulation. They have their greedy snouts in so many hog buckets they are finding it hard to spot new hog buckets, safe, profitable investment opportunities in which to sink all the excess cash. There are three solutions to this financial dilemma. Preparations for war. War itself and privatization of government institutions and public utilities. War is good for business. Since 1945 the United States has been involved in five major wars and got their asses kicked in four of them. But win or lose they all turned a good profit. Investing in the arms industry is always a safe bet. Still, even that isn't enough. The shadowy 199 are determined to privatise everything, schools, prisons, power plants, the police, post offices, the military, water, sewage and parks, anything out of which they can wring a profit. This concentration of wealth is terrifying. The consequences catastrophic for the working class. People are quick enough to riot over racial injustice, transgender rights and other social issues. So why aren't people screaming out in protest at what Uncle Scrooge and the big banks are doing? Why aren't they marching on the headquarters of these seventeen financial giants? Why aren't they scaring the shit of out the 199 that hold the destiny of 7.8 billion lives in the palms of their grubby, greedy hands? The drums of revolution are beating throughout the world, but they are beating for the wrong reasons, identifying the wrong enemies.

There are plenty of explanations for this alarming apathy. Finance and economics are difficult and boring subjects to the average person. They don't understand them. Economics only touches their lives when the price of food and other essentials goes up. Or when the company they work for goes bust and they are thrown out of work, standing outside the locked factory gates unemployed, broke and bewildered. Otherwise, the financial news makes them yawn. And no wonder. Most of it is nothing more than press releases issued by the financial giants. The bullshit they want us to swallow. It's all Pablum and propaganda. The real story is never told. The truth is smothered by deceptive newscasts, happy sitcoms, soapy dramas, cop programs, sporting events and cheesy game shows to keep us distracted and entertained.

The financial elites that run the world are the merciless robber barons of the 21st century. Their greed is richly rewarded and their crimes are never punished. In their unholy quest for more and more wealth they are destroying the planet, stirring up wars and rumours of wars, brainwashing us with their media propaganda and arousing hatred and sedition among the poor and the marginalised. There is a strong possibility that the Corona pandemic will trigger the next financial collapse. This is still unclear. But one thing is for sure. The pandemic will make the rich obscenely richer. Huge government bailouts to save favoured industries such as the airlines will be lavished on the criminal bankers, asset managers and CEO's whose avarice and short-sightedness makes the next collapse inevitable.

41

THE BANKING CASINO AND ITS CROOKED CROUPIERS

IN THE 1920's there was an outrageous New York nightclub hostess called Texas Guillian who greeted her customers with the welcoming words: "Hello suckers." Those cheery words should be placed over the door of every giant international bank and financial corporation. Because that's what we are – suckers!

We are hoodwinked into swallowing the lie that banks are responsible institutions. That they exist to serve the community. That they are honest and open in their dealings. That the loans they make are secure. That they are efficient and never make terrible blunders. That they operate under strict moral and financial codes. That it's not just gambling with other people's money. That they actually know what they are doing.

The history of banking tells a very different tale. Banks from the Medici's all the way down to Lehman Brothers have always been gambling casinos. They always lend more than they hold in reverse, gambling that depositors won't arrive all at once demanding their money. They gamble on risky investments, hoping they will pay off. They use profits and bailouts to buy back their own stock, raising their share price on Wall Street, enriching their investors, and awarding themselves huge salary hikes and eye-watering bonuses. They invent and sell new financial instruments that prove to be worthless. They created the subprime mortgage bubble and then gorged themselves on the government bailouts. They roll the dice every day and aren't above cheating and fraud.

Since the crash of 2008 there have been no shortage of banking scandals. In 2016 Wells Fargo was fined $185 million for creating new accounts for customers without bothering to tell the customers about their new, unasked for accounts. In 2018 Us Bancorp was fined $613 million for alleged money laundering. In Australia five of the nation's largest banks have been caught collecting fees for services they never provided. Banks around the world have been investigated and fined for price fixing. In 2017 Wells Fargo was at it again. This time in a car insurance swindle. JPMorgan Chase, USB, Barclay's PLC and Citibank have all paid massive fines for criminal activities. These crooked bankers are slicker than snot on a doorknob, too slimy to catch. They are never punished. They never go to prison.

After the terrible stock market crash in 1929, President Roosevelt put the mad dog banks and the out-of-control stock market on a tight leash. He regulated them until they screamed. He put an end to Wild West financial speculation, but he couldn't put an end to the great depression caused by the crash. It took the Second World War to get America booming again. Now, 75 years later, Roosevelt's sensible reforms have long been dumped. The mad dog bankers and the rapacious stock market is off the leash again, free to cheat, swindle, break the law and ignore what little regulation remains.

The giant banks are supposed to be in competition with each other. This is yet another lie. Their interlocking networks makes competition unprofitable. They work in concert to promote mutual interests, share investment opportunities and forge risk agreements. They use their combined power to create a political climate favourable to white collar crime and financial skulduggery.

We are told these huge, financial institutions

are too big to fail. But we aren't told why they were allowed to get so big in the first place. That would expose the corruption of the whole rotten system. Uncle Scrooge pulls the political strings. Uncle Scrooge sends lobbyist to Washington to pressure elected officials, and even write the legislation he wants enacted, bills to deregulate and cut corporate taxes. Uncle Scrooge discourages criminal investigations and positively forbids embarrassing prosecutions. Uncle Scrooge along with the asset managers and the CEO's of transnational companies are the ruling elite, the protected elite. They are the criminals who never face justice.

They know their crimes are likely to be exposed sooner or later. Illegally-inflated profits, price fixing, criminal practices, money laundering, huge losses and cooked books can't be hidden forever. But they also know they won't go to jail. Their friends in government and the judiciary will see to that. Most of the time they never even face trial. They are permitted to keep their money and property. Getting slapped with a fine and being allowed to resign with an obscene golden handshake is the worst that will happen. Their punishment for causing financial devastation to thousands of ordinary people is a lavish retirement on a sunny, private beach and playing golf at some exclusive club. These insatiable swine couldn't care less about the lives they've ruined.

Uncle Scrooge runs the casino and all the wheels are rigged. The rest of us are just suckers who naively believed the house was honest.

42

AMERICA IS DROWNING NOT WAVING

AMERICA IS NOW the boss country of the world. It's been the boss since the end of the Second World War. For 75 years Uncle Sam has been throwing his weight around. He exploits weak and poor countries in every corner of the earth. He overthrows foreign governments he doesn't like. He assassinates heads of state that stand in the way of American dominance. He invades sovereign nations in undeclared wars and four out of five times comes out with a bloody nose followed by a humiliating kick up the ass.

Uncle Sam is a bully. Since the 1970's America has been a bad boss country, a shabby, cruel, hated world leader using force, or the threat of force, both economic and military, to achieve its global ambitions. Now the chickens are coming home to roost. Uncle Sam is in bad health. His leaders are incompetent and dishonest. His infrastructure is crumbling. His inner cities are slums. His education system broken. His lead in technology lost. His countryside is ravished, his borders open, his industries trashed and shipped overseas and there are race riots in the streets. American citizens are angry, fearful, impoverished, unemployed, drug-addicted, violent and bewildered.

So, what happened? Where did it all go wrong? America was once the shining light of the world. It was a nation created on the premise that all men were created equal. America was another name for freedom and opportunity. "Give me your poor, your huddled masses..." was an open invitation to the world's ragged, oppressed immigrants flooding through Ellis Island to begin a new life in the Promised Land.

The seeds of the American decline were planted during the great depression of the 1930's. People were starving, homeless, demoralised and angry. The smell of insurrection was in the wind. Representatives of the working class went to see the president, Franklin Delano Roosevelt. They told Franklin that if something wasn't done to help the people there would certainly be a revolution just as there was in Russia in 1917. Franklin was a very smart man, one of the best presidents America ever had, including George Washington and Honest Abe. He understood the gravity of the situation and he agreed to help the people provided all this dangerous revolutionary agitation was stopped. A deal was done. Franklin went to the bankers and the rich elites and read them the riot act. He warned them that if they didn't sit still for tremendous tax hikes the country was doomed, they would lose everything and end up hanging from a lamppost on Fifth Avenue. The Uncle Scrooges gave in, but not without screams of rage and howls of protest.

Franklin called his economic program of reforms The New Deal. He taxed the shit out of the rich and put the country back to work building roads, bridges, dams and houses. He set up a welfare system and strengthened the labour movement. He saved the country and became the most popular president ever, serving an unprecedented fourth term, during which he died.

Once the Second World War was out of the way, the Uncle Scrooges struck back. They went to work undoing everything the hated Roosevelt had done. They began with the labour unions, using their government lackeys to enact legislation undermining union power to the point where they had no power at all. Then they attacked welfare, cutting it to the bone. They engineered huge tax breaks for themselves. They got fatter, richer and more powerful as the years went on. By 2008, when the subprime mortgage bubble burst, it was as if Roosevelt had never existed. America was firmly back in the hands of the rapacious Uncle Scrooges. Reforms, like everything else, have a limited life span.

Today, as I speak, we are in a similar situation. The corona virus has devastated the economy. Millions have died. Businesses of all kinds shut their doors for good. Millions more were thrown out of work. Prices are rising and the unemployed have no money to buy groceries, or pay their rent. The situation is dire. America needs another Franklin Roosevelt to lead the country out of this crisis. And who does it have? Sleepy Joe Biden, a senile, corrupt, incompetent, uninformed buffoon who thinks his wife is the vice president. This is beyond satire. Even Jonathan Swift couldn't make it up.

The pandemic has put another hole in an already sinking ship. There is no great leader waiting in the wings to save America. The republican reptiles and the disgraceful democrats are two branches of the same poison tree. They are two elites in conflict, more interested in destroying each other than in saving the country. Above them are the controlling financial elites pulling the strings and ghoulishly bloating themselves on the carcass of the American dream.

Like a species of wasp they have laid their eggs in the body politic of America and the hatchlings have hollowed it out from the inside. For a nation to call itself great it must be successful in war. The American military reminds me of Primo Canera, the ambling Alp, a muscular giant who briefly reigned as the world heavyweight boxing champion in the early 1930's. Primo was huge and menacing. He looked the part, but he couldn't box and he couldn't punch. When he came up against a real fighter in defence of his phony title, Primo got his jaw broken, his nose flattened and his ass kicked. This happens all the time to the American military. It picks a fight, gets its nose broken, its head punched in and crawls away in a humiliating defeat. Think of Korea, Vietnam, the Middle East and Afghanistan. Another sure sign of a nation's decline is a drop in life expectancy. The life expectancy of the average American is going down, not up. The American health care system is one of the worst and the most expensive in the world and the recent pandemic has swept the country like the Black Death.

The heady days of the 50's and 60's have long gone. The last great president America had was Lyndon Baines Johnson, LBJ, a man who dedicated his entire life to becoming the President of the United States. He was a flawed human being, a bully, a liar, a bribe-taker and perhaps a murderer. He wanted power, money and women. It was said he had a huge penis which he called 'Jumbo' and had no hesitation about pulling it out and wiggling it at any woman he wanted to fuck. He hated the Kennedys, especially Bobby – who hated him right back. He was jealous of their privileged background and easy success. He resented Jack's reputation as a lover when he knew he'd fucked more women than Jack had hot dinners. Lyndon Johnson was not a nice man. He was born poor and clawed his way up from the dirt of the Texas hill country. Yet, for all his faults he, a southerner, tried to do more for the blacks and the poor than any president since Roosevelt. Johnson called his package of reforms The Great Society. But he wasn't popular and he wasn't lucky. Kennedy left him a deadly legacy – the Vietnam War and racial unrest – which ruined his presidency and his popularity. American cities were burning. The war was going badly. Protesters gathered in front of the White House chanting: "Hey, Hey, LBJ, how many babies did you kill today?" He resigned in despair after one term and died on his Texas ranch with that horrible chant echoing in his ear. The republican wrecking crew soon reduced The Great Society to rubble just as they had the New Deal.

The American presidents that followed were disappointing, mediocre or corrupt. Probably the most disappointing was Barack Obama who came to power on a great wave of enthusiasm and hope. He was another Jack Kennedy, handsome, articulate and charming. A clean-cut family man who, unlike Kennedy, didn't play around. And even better he was a man of colour. Change was on the way. African Americans would finally get the justice and equality they deserved. It didn't happen. Obama was a damp squib. He preferred playing golf with his rich friends to addressing the urgent problem of the American decline. Like Kennedy he was all image, a fake, a front man, the acceptable face of Wall Street avarice.

Welcome sleepy Joe Biden, a stale left-over from the moribund Obama administration. Arguably, Joe is the worst president the American people have ever had. He has trouble finding his way to the Oval Office, let alone leading the free world. Uncle Sam is mighty sick. The average duration of an empire is two hundred and fifty years. Some last longer. Others appear briefly and then fall apart. The Nazi Empire only lasted twelve years. The Japanese Empire a mere fourteen. The Russian Empire less than a century. Today, the American empire finds itself facing many of the same problems as the Roman Empire in the third century. Uncontrolled immigration in the form of barbarian invasions, incessant civil unrest and a worsening economic crisis. The Roman Empire was saved by one man, the emperor, Diocletian. When he came to power, Rome was on its knees. He saved Rome. He made Rome great again.

An American collapse isn't as inevitable as some doom-mongers predict. When a nation is in deep trouble it occasionally throws up a strong leader. The German crisis threw up Hitler. The Russian revolution produced Lenin. Britain in the 70's was all but washed up, the sick man of Europe. Margaret Thatcher reversed all that. Great leaders are not always good people, but they are tough, determined people who know how to get things done. America has faced crises before. The Civil War produced Abraham Lincoln. The Great Depression, Franklin Roosevelt. America is a great nation capable of renewal, but it needs a hero, a leader to show it a way out of the valley of death.

43

Boots and Saddles: The American Military Machine

The American Republic was born in the blood and fire of war. And it has been at war ever since. For 227 of the last 244 years America has been fighting a war somewhere in the world. From the time of its birth in 1776 until the present day it has enjoyed a mere 17 years of peace. The United States is a violent country, awash with guns and plagued by mass shootings. Americans loved the idea of war until Vietnam demonstrated what it actually cost. News of American atrocities in Vietnam shocked the public. When the body bags began to arrive back home the American love of war dried up like a puddle of piss in the Texas sun.

And yet the wars went on. The endless War on Terror, The Gulf War, Iraq, Afghanistan. Of the five major wars the United States has fought since 1945 it got its ass kicked in four of them. America, has forgotten how to win wars and learned to lose as expensively as it can.

How is this possible? The United States is the most powerful nation in the history of the world. In terms of military muscle, it stands head and shoulders above its nearest rival. The United States maintains 800 bases in 70 countries around the world at the cost of many billions of dollars. Yet it loses war after war and never seems to achieve its strategic aims. It is without equal and without victory. So why does Uncle Sam do it? Why does he waste so much treasure and so many lives sticking his nose where it doesn't belong?

The American military isn't there to protect freedom at home and abroad. It is the enforcer of American big business. It is there to protect American interests in nasty, dangerous places where they don't want Coca Cola and quarter pounders. It struts around the world carrying a big stick and saying: "You'll drink our Cokes and eat our hamburgers or else!" The American power elite use the armed forces to intimidate weaker nations, to discourage resistance to their capitalist agenda and to consolidate their investments around the world. America's frequent intrusions into other countries are usually justified as humanitarian peacekeeping missions. But the truth is those resistant populations are refusing to guzzle their Cokes and choke down their big macs. Young American soldiers die on foreign streets in faraway places to serve the ignoble purposes of Wall Street and the big banks.

Intelligence agencies are also servants of the financial elites. They work hand in glove with the military to insure the uninterrupted flow of money from the world's poorest regions to the bulging pockets of the super-rich. The CIA is busy in every country in the world sniffing out threats to American interests. Uncooperative regimes are undermined and overthrown. The CIA spreads disinformation, sows discontent, assassinates troublesome leaders, drums up revolutionary movements and replaces elected officials with psychopathic dictators eager to collaborate in the rape of their own nation. At home they act with more restraint. They hire PR firms to smear their enemies, and gangsters to do the dirty work. The CIA is a terrorist organization in all but name.

The American financial elite don't stop there. When the military and the intelligence agencies are slow to respond they have private security firms to take up the slack. These security companies offer a wide range of services. They provide protection for the top men and women and their families. They guarantee safe work zones. They guard banks and private buildings. They gather intelligence and are capable of outright warfare if necessary. Security firms are big business. They employ 15 million people worldwide. They have their own well-equipped armies and were heavily involved in Iraq and Afghanistan assisting the military and themselves in a number of lucrative ways. These companies are the hired guns of capitalism. In 2007 the gunslingers went berserk and shot and killed 17 innocent Iraqis in a Baghdad square. There was a big stink, but nothing much changed except the private security industry has grown in power, stature and importance. No wonder the Arabs burn the American flag in the streets of their war-torn cities. The Great Satan has pissed all over them.

Yet, for all its might the US military is failing. It has four different arms. The army, the navy, the air force and the marines. These are elites within an elite and are in fierce competition with one another for government funding and securing their own power bases. A military officer's career depends on commanding fantastically expensive and complex weapons systems that are no good for the kind of wars being fought in the 21st century. Weapons contracts to private manufactures give the Uncle Scrooges and the generals a shared interest in high military spending. The generals know these new weapons systems are the wrong weapons, but they don't care. Low-tech weapons designed for actual combat don't interest them. An American general will lay down his life for his country, but he won't lay down his career. Keeping his rank and command is much more important than what's good for the security of his country. Their precious weapons systems also provide a lucrative retirement. Grateful defence firms often hire redundant officers at high salaries as a kind of pay-off for their cooperation.

The military elite is perversely damaging its own fighting ability. Buying weapons that are too expensive, too quickly produced, too indiscriminate, too cumbersome to manoeuvre and too powerful to use in a real war is a prescription for failure.

All this fancy, overpriced weaponry creates the belief that America can kick the shit out of anybody. This foolish over-confidence leads military and civilian leaders to loose the dogs of war with the usual disastrous result. US troops arrive with no understanding of the place they are invading, little training in counter-insurgency and carrying the wrong weapons into a war already lost. When everything starts to go wrong, the commanders order up more firepower which does nothing but piss off the local population even more. Defeat and humiliation are inevitable.

The American war machine is a lumbering, top-heavy giant. In 2012 it had 945 generals and admirals on active duty. Only the year before they added another 93. That's one flag-rank officer for every 1,500 soldiers. This is the stuff of comedy. If this trend continues there will three generals to every tank and six admirals to every ship. The air force will naturally demand parity.

Another huge problem for the American military is the public's refusal to accept high casualty figures. Unfortunately, war produces body bags in large numbers. It requires troops willing to die for the cause. Americans seem strangely reluctant to die for the cause of Wall Street and Goldman Sachs. During their disastrous wars American generals always point to the high death count they inflict on the enemy as a sign of ultimate victory. As usual they got it ass backwards. What it actually shows is the enemy's fanatical commitment to drive out the hated Americans at any cost. Their eager willingness to fight and die for a just cause, for freedom, for self-determination. The American troops, on the other hand, have no clear idea of what they are fighting for, or why they are dying in some distant shithole they couldn't point to on a map.

America is the only superpower left standing.

The biggest beast in the jungle. It reminds me of a lumbering elephant in a world seething with killer ants. No matter how many it steps on, millions of others will swarm over the great beast and eventually eat it alive.

44

THE WASHINGTON SNAKE PIT

FOR SOME REASON this dream city was built in the middle of a swamp and something of the swamp, a clammy corruption and the odour of rot perseveres to this very day. My purpose in this essay is to take a look at some of the slithering animal life that lurks in the swamp.

The two main political parties, the republican reptiles and the disgraceful democrats are locked in a deadly struggle to destroy one another. They are so busy tearing each other apart they have little time for governing the country. Governing is an annoying distraction. Congressmen and women let the lobbyists write the legislation while they plot and plan to destroy the enemy party. When I think of the republican reptiles and the disgraceful democrats I picture two selfish, corrupt old men fighting to the death over the last potato in the setting sun of a dying planet.

Meanwhile, over at the White House, sleepy Joe is dozing in the Oval Office pleased with the way he's managed the Covid-19 pandemic and the withdrawal from Afghanistan. The US has recorded more pandemic deaths than any other country on earth. America is number one! The top spot! Quite an achievement, Joe. Still, the country faces terrible problems. Forty million unemployed. An economic meltdown far worse than 2008 staring him in the face. Is Joe worried? Hell, no. He knows how to fix it. He'll bailout the big boys, the banks, the airlines and the defence industries and tell the people, who will get nothing, he's giving trillions of dollars to the super-rich to save the country. He likes to lie big.

He's far more concerned with gender politics, masking mandates and trying to remember what day it is than he is about solving the country's problems. On Capitol Hill the politicians are lousy with parasites called lobbyists. These loathsome snakes in suits slither into the inviting orifices of elected officials and take them over completely. The snakes have no loyalties, no honour and no scruples. They'll work for anyone with the money to pay. This includes foreign governments, shady Russian moguls, Chinese trade negotiators and the billionaire American ruling class who seek to subvert democracy and control the political process on the sly.

While American citizens relax at home in front of the TV, the snakes are chipping away at the very foundations on which America was built. Every morning the American citizen wakes up unaware that there is a little less of America than there was the day before.

Most Americans believe they live in a democracy. They don't. Democracy is a carefully crafted illusion that conceals the ugly truth. Americans live in something called an oligarchy. A country ruled by a small clique of vampire billionaires who control the legislative process through their parasitic lobbyists in Washington. No law gets passed that will threaten the power and wealth of the oligarchs. The only laws that get passed are those that enhance their wealth and tighten their strangle-hold on power. Every now and then a bone is thrown to the bewildered masses, generally around election time.

What does America have in common with China, Iran, Saudi Arabia, Turkey and Russia? They are all oligarchies. They are all ruled by small, rapacious elites. Their political systems might be wildly different, but their ideology and objectives are exactly the same. To get richer and hang on to power at all costs. Oligarchies can flourish in a monarchy, in a democracy and in a dictatorship. They exist for no other reason than to concentrate their wealth and to perpetuate their class.

As I speak there are some 12,000 lobbyists trying to slither into the orifices of 535 Washington politicians elected to govern the country. That's about 22.4 lobbyists for every senator and congress-person in Washington. No wonder these elected officials squirm and scurry so much. So many freebies. So little time. The free meals in expensive restaurants. Tickets to sporting events, concerts and other cultural happenings. Golf junkets to exotic locations, bulging brown envelopes for the retirement fund and most important of all, campaign contributions. And all for a few, harmless legislative favours.

Your average Washington politician comes pretty cheap considering what he or she has to offer. Like the bishops of old they have been given the power to bind or to loose. Or to put it into more modern terms: to regulate, or deregulate, to tax or not to tax. The bishops of old consulted God before coming to a decision. Washington politicians consult their lobbyists and then back deregulation and tax cuts for the rich. America! The land of the freebie and the home of the depraved.

But there is another America. It lies in the ignored, so called fly-over states between the power centres of the east and west coasts. This vast middle ground is full of desperate, bewildered people wondering what happened. Why am I out of work? Why am I so deep in debt? Why do I have three mortgages on the house? The country they knew and loved seemed to disappear overnight. They went to bed in America and woke up in Venezuela.

They woke up to the fact that they had been betrayed, sold out by their cheap, sleazy representatives in Washington. When Donald Trump cried: "Let's make America great again!" these people dreamed of a golden age, a time of full employment, affordable housing, a new car every couple of years and even a college education for their kids that didn't incur crippling debt. There was a time when all that was possible. And they wanted that time back again.

When Donald Trump promised to drain the swamp they wanted desperately to believe him. They knew Washington was a snake pit full of greed and corruption. The ignored majority wanted revenge: jail sentences, politicians in orange jumpsuits. Donald Trump divided America. Sleepy Joe promised to unite the nation. But all the nation got was more of the same. Joe Biden is a man who has risen several levels above his natural level of incompetence. He's unfit to be president of the United States. Everyone knows it but him. A credible opponent could easily unseat him in the 2024 election. So who is this credible opponent, the shining hope of the Republican Party?

Is a rematch with Donald Trump in the offing? Such a contest would be black comedy, a titanic mismatch between two very different septuagenarians, the feeble versus the ferocious. It won't be pretty to watch.

Trump has been written off too many times and won against all the odds not to be taken seriously. All his blundering, buffoonery and blustering seems to make no difference. All his lies, broken promises and incompetence makes no difference. Trump could well return for a second term. Another chance to make America ridiculous again.

The Washington snake pit is alive and writhing with poisonous serpents. The swamp is bigger than ever. And what of democracy? Oh, that passed away quietly in the 1980's and nobody noticed.

PART TEN

Fear and Loathing

45

THE GREENING OF SELF-PITY CITY

How did the culture of victimhood begin? How did a weepy place like Self-Pity City come to rise up from the hard soil of stoicism and pioneer self-reliance? Who laid the first stone? Who shed the first tear?

The founding father of cry-baby culture was a ragged loafer called Jean Jacques Rousseau. Jean was born in Geneva in 1712 and spent a large portion of his life as a wandering vagabond, a parasitic tramp living on the charity of others hardly less destitute than himself. When death finally dried his tears in Paris in 1778, he'd become one of the most famous men in Europe.

A sage, a prophet, a worthy rival of the great Voltaire. By the relaxed standards of the 18th century Rousseau was deemed to be a philosopher. Rational thought wasn't for him. His appeal was to the heart, not the brain.

It was Rousseau, not Marx, who wrote the immortal line. *Man is born free, and everywhere he is in chains.* Rousseau is the father of the Romantic Movement that swept through Europe in the 18th and early 19th centuries and utterly changed the way people saw the world. His effect on philosophy, religion, politics and literature was enormous. He made self-pity not only acceptable, but fashionable. He placed sensitivity and emotion above everything else. Tears above testosterone. Reason, he preached, was the cause of everything that was wrong with the world. Feeling, not thinking, should lead the way forward. Foolishness and faith should be exalted. Science and rational thought strangled and done away with. He wanted to throw all the achievements of the enlightenment in the ash can and, like Pol Pot and Islamic fundamentalists, turn the clock back to the year zero.

The rejection of reason in favour of the heart fell on fertile ground. Stiff upper lips were quivering. People were sick of reason. They had a belly-full of the enlightenment. Reason was too stifling, too sensible, too ridged, too demanding, too difficult. Reason was always saying no. And reason was destroying the world as they knew it. It had brought something called the industrial revolution. Blake's 'dark satanic mills' were filling the meadows with slag heaps, blackening the skies overhead and the towns below. Reason was making human hands and human skill redundant. The old trades were disappearing and it was all the fault of reason. Reason created the gloom and the despair that hung over the bleak industrial landscapes of Rousseau's time.

Rousseau gave people a new appreciation of natural beauty. Before Rousseau men viewed the land simply as productive. Fields of waving wheat and corn, pastures filled with lowing cattle were beautiful. The rest was just waste. Rousseau opened their eyes to the beauty of nature in the raw. Of empty fields blazing with wildflowers. Of dark, pathless forests and the forbidding slopes of lofty, snow-peaked Alps. He was Swiss after all. He pointed out things of such unnoticed beauty that it brought a sob of wonder.

He also gave us the Noble Savage, man living in the state of nature, uncorrupted by civilization, untroubled by greed and unspoiled by education. The Noble Savage needs no book learning. He is born wise, innately virtuous, a loving husband, a gentle father, a good provider and the follower of a religion that oozes natural kindness. Anthropologists would be surprised to discover such a creature. Cannibals and head-hunters live by a different creed.

Rousseau even changed the way we think about God. Before Rousseau theologians offered intellectual explanations to prove the existence of God. Rousseau hated all the old proofs, the products of logic and intellectual thought. He argued that reason could no more explain God than it could explain the world we live in. The human intellect was incapable of solving such metaphysical mysteries. Instead, we must forget logical reasoning. New instruments of perception must be found. Desire, need, instinct, feelings and emotions were the new instruments Rousseau chose. Reason was replaced with awe and wonder at the beauty and complexity of the world around us. The proof of God could be found in a blade of grass, or a grain of sand. God lives in our hearts, not in our heads. This way of thinking has become so prevalent that we don't realise what a startling change it was.

In the field of literature he inspired Byron, Keats, Shelly, Coleridge and Wordsworth. The German Shakespeare, Wolfgang von Goethe, penned a best-selling tear-jerker called *The Sorrows of Young Werther*. The hero of this gloomy romance was a whining, love-sick weakling obsessed by a woman engaged to another man.

Werther makes feeble attempts to seduce her and she firmly rejects him. The whole story consists of Werther sobbing and weeping over his lost love. He is plunged into romantic despair. He is inconsolable with grief and self-pity. He can't stand the pain. He wants to murder someone, but he is too sensitive to kill his fantasy woman, or her fiancé. So he turns a gun on himself and blows out his brains, ending his life with a whimper.

This soap-opera weepy sold like hotcakes. It became a sensation. All over Europe young lovesick fools were killing themselves in imitation of Werther. This sort of story has had a long shelf-life. It still flourishes in our own day. Movies like *Leaving Las Vegas* are still packing them in. *Leaving Las Vegas* is a particularly repulsive example of the genre. It's about another weakling, an alcoholic this time, who lacks the character and the willpower to kick the bottle. So what does he do to solve his problem? Join AA? That's not what cry-babies do. They embrace their problem and parade their self-pity for all the world to see. Our drunken hero heads for the world capital of vulgarity to drink himself to death, to commit suicide by bartender. Instead of sobbing like young Werther, this juice-head is chugging down the booze in physically impossible amounts. No human being could drink that much alcohol. I know. I've tried. Eventually, our stumble-bum hero gets involved with another loser, a broken-down hooker with a heart of gold. There's nothing like doomed love to get the tears flowing. By the end of the movie there's not a dry eye in the house. Our intoxicated hero dies a sodden wreck in the arms of his low-rent hooker. A three-hanky weepie. I was sobbing too. But it was sobs of laughter.

The message of the film is clear. Not even love is strong enough to overcome the might of self-pity. Losers and weaklings can become heroes too if they die romantically. A manipulated audience is seduced into sympathising with these despicable cretins, swallowing the sugar-coated message of victimhood and buying into the noble virtue of self-pity. The brave, daring hero of yesteryear has been buried in an unmarked grave, replaced by the cry-baby who squalls at every little hurt.

We have Rousseau to thank for all of that. This apostle of sensitivity, this champion of the teardrop was, in reality, a monumental hypocrite, not a good or a kindly man. He repaid kindness with the blackest ingratitude. He was a master of the sob story. He knew how to squeeze out a tear. He lived on the sympathy of others. When he was caught stealing ribbons from a rich lady he worked for, Rousseau blamed the crime on the hapless serving girl for whom he'd stolen the ribbons. He was released without charge. She went to jail. When his ignorant drudge of a mistress presented him with five children he didn't want he quickly got rid of them. As each baby was born he took it from its mother and deposited it on the door-step of the foundling hospital, which in those days was a sentence of death. This philosopher of feelings, this promoter of sentiment and the tender heart, proved to be selfish, dishonest, ruthless and cruel. Yet he understood the power of tears. He built the sturdy, hypocritical foundations on which Self-Pity City rests. He is the father of today's spoiled cry-babies whose tears threaten to wash away western civilization. Jean Jacques Rousseau had no heart to call his own. He was utterly heartless. But his ideas touched the hearts of millions.

46

THE TWILIGHT OF THE IDOLS

THE IDOLS ARE coming down everywhere. Iconoclasm has again busted loose. Statues of the great and the good are being ripped from their pedestals, pissed on, splattered with paint, broken up and dumped in the drink. The lynching of statues is nothing new. It's been going on for thousands of years, People have been tearing them down since governments started putting them up to honour the nation's heroes.

The attack on statues is an assault on the prevailing hierarchy. It is a declaration that the authority of the current leadership is no longer recognised. It is demand for change. A howl of rage at existing conditions. A rejection of the existing order and an explicit threat to the ruling class. You could be next.

The authorities have two choices: force or capitulation. Call in the riot squad, or kneel to the demands. Mobs have no interest in compromise. Both courses are fraught with danger. Brute force could arouse more anger, more riots and in some cases lead to full-blown revolt. Capitulation, on the other hand, is equally dangerous. It could be perceived as weakness and embolden the mob to further demands and more destructive disorders.

In the current spate of disturbances the authorities have chosen to kneel, bow their heads and beg forgiveness for crimes they never committed. I look at this gutless pack of shivering cowards and almost sympathise with the mob. Such quislings don't deserve to be in charge of anything. Kneeling to the mob is a sure way to turn a democracy into a crimeocracy, and then into a tyranny.

Mobs and capitalism have two things in common. Both need growth to sustain themselves. And both feel persecuted and under threat from enemy forces out to destroy them. Mobs enjoy burning houses, cars and small businesses. Of all the forces of destruction the most impressive is fire. It can be seen from far away and it attracts more people to join the mob. There is something satisfying in the sounds of splintering wood, smashed glass and the crackle and snap of a burning house. It is the cry of fresh life, of something new being born.

A frontier has been crossed, a line erased, the boundary between the public and the private broken down. The shop filled with goods intended for sale now belongs to everyone. The mob doesn't see looting as a crime. Grabbing that colour TV is an expression of liberation. So is the destruction of buildings, cars and statues. Free at last. Free at last.

Riots always begin with an outrage of some sort committed by the authorities. A crowd gathers and marches in protest. Some are there to get justice, some have a political agenda and some are out for excitement and loot, violence and fire. The rest are the guilt-ridden hitchhikers thumbing a ride on a worthy cause, any cause.

There is a distance between people that disappears in a crowd. Differences in status, intelligence, education and all the other things that separate people melt away. You are no longer an individual. You have become a part of something bigger. Distances close. There is a great relief in letting go, of losing one's self in the mass.

Crowds are particularly sensitive to feelings of persecution. They have a natural urge for growth. Anything that tries to prevent that growth is an enemy. No matter what the authorities do it will be regarded as a hostile act, or a trick to break up the crowd. One wrong move on either side is enough to kick it off. The crowd becomes a mob and the looting and the burning begins. Only when the flames die away and the last burning building has collapsed does the mob drift away back to individual lives full of boredom, anxiety and discontent.

When the crowd is part of a movement to change society the disturbances will continue until the aims of the movement are met. Or the movement is crushed. The success of a movement depends on its appeal to the crowd. Crowds can draw strength from the most ridiculous sources – a slogan, a word, a button, or a T-shirt. All mass movements point to the future. They put their faith in it. They promise change and they peddle hope. The young are full of hope. They hope for a better, brighter future. So do the minorities and other disadvantaged groups. The movement swells from a worthy cause, into something much more frightening: a holy cause.

Comfortable middle-class people over forty abhor and fear the crowd. When hopes and dreams are loose in the streets the timid lock their doors and windows and lie low until the madness passes. They fear the future and hate the thought of change. They cling to the present because it is safe. The future is an undiscovered country full of menace and uncertainty. And change is always change for the worse. Holy causes are the most terrifying of all. They throw open the stable doors to free the four horsemen of the apocalypse. War, pestilence, famine and death ride high on holy causes.

The leaders of these movements are usually thrown up by the crowd. The men who started the French Revolution had no political experience. Neither did the Bolsheviks, the Nazis or the revolutionaries in Asia. Only later when a movement is up and running does the experienced man of affairs enter the picture to offer advice, support and money.

The Black Lives Matter movement has swelled up into a holy cause. Black Lives Matter is a brilliant slogan. Pure genius. How could anyone who is not a racist disagree? Black Lives Matter is a self-evident truth that can't be disputed. However, one crucial word has been omitted. 'Only'. The rest of us are exculded. At a football match in Britain the players, black and white, were obediently taking the knee for Black Lives Matter when a light plane began circling overhead trailing a banner that said: White Lives Matter. This caused an outrage. The police were quickly on the case. They soon tracked the odious heretic down, but were angry and frustrated when they couldn't find an offense to charge him with. Still he was severely punished for this non-offense. He was banned from his local football ground for life and fired from his job. The man had broken no law. He'd done nothing wrong except state a less popular truth. He was punished, but not nearly enough. Clearly, new legislation is needed to deal with this sort of blasphemy.

So far the well-funded Black Lives Matter movement has thrown up no charismatic leader like Malcolm X, or Martin Luther King Jr. Without such a leader the movement will fracture and eventually fizzle out like the Black Panthers and the Symbiones Liberation Army. The conditions are ripe for such a leader to emerge. Paranoia, fear, uncertainty and distrust are in the air. Pestilence, one of the four horsemen of the apocalypse, is already loose and killing multitudes everywhere. The other horsemen could soon follow. Economic collapse and a devastating depression is on the way. The authorities are hopelessly incompetent and weak. People are nervous, angry and looking for something to blame. Even more urgently they are looking for something to believe in. Yes, the conditions are ripe for a new Malcom X to take the stage.

Black Lives Matter has revealed itself to be a hard-left revolutionary movement. It shows signs of wanting to overthrow democracy and replace capitalism with something else. What began as a protest movement, a movement for social justice, has become something threatening and dangerous. Holy causes have a way of turning into social nightmares.

In the meantime the massacre of the statues will go on. Stained-glass windows will be next, followed by museums forced to remove suspect pieces. Then street names. The authorities will cravenly cave in to every outrageous demand. The chancellors of universities and the curators of museums will do nothing to stop it. Neither will city mayors, state governors, or luminaries like the Archbishop of Canterbury who will nod with approval at the defaced churches he is supposed to protect. All that will remain will be the empty plinths, the gaping windows, the looted museums and the bemused people searching for street names that no longer exist. Vandalised urban landscapes will be the memento muri to remind us of what we've lost to the power of the mob and to the cowardice of our gutless leaders.

47

ALL THE HEROES HAVE LEFT THE BUILDING

THE WORD 'HERO' has lost its meaning. In the old days a hero was a man of destiny chosen by the gods for some great task: to found a city, build a nation, start a new religion or to lead an oppressed people to freedom as Moses did the Jews. The history of humanity is the biography of the great men and women who stood out from the crowd and moved the world forward. Heroes are men and women who not only changed history, but made history. Heroes come in a variety of roles. The warrior, the prophet, the saint, the lover, the world redeemer, the priest and the poet. In order to fulfil his destiny the hero had to endure many trials, slay many monsters, overcome many obstacles and face many tests of strength and ingenuity before the goal is reached. If this sounds like the plot of a Hollywood super-hero movie it is. One we've all seen many times.

Comic-book heroes have replaced the real thing. So have celebrities who are often mistaken for heroes. Bill Cosby was such a hero. Remember him? Everybody wants to be a hero. Everyone dreams of doing some heroic deed and receiving the fame and adulation it would bring. But in our hearts we know it will never happen. We know we will die unheroic deaths, lie in unvisited graves and moulder away in uncelebrated solitude.

Perhaps that's why so many famous faces try to make the leap from forgettable celebrity to bone-fide hero. Unlike the rest of us they have the great advantage of being well-known. That gives them a platform. But how to make the leap? What cause to support? What holy crusade will give them an aura of heroism? Celebrities of colour inevitably go to bat for the race/equality issue. So do grovelling white celebrities eager to parade their Woke credentials, but they always look a little uncomfortable, slightly shame-faced whenever they speak out on the subject of race. They must step carefully. One wrong adjective could be fatal. I suspect activists of colour look upon these white, guilt-ridden hitchhikers with contempt, just as Stalin did western intellectuals who supported Communism in the 30's. Useful idiots, he called them. There's never been any shortage of those.

The great-grandsons of these useful idiots are alive and well and working hard to destroy capitalism and democracy. They hate western civilization. They hate the very culture that bred them because the politically correct education system has taught them to do so. It has taught them to despise their white history and the white men and women who made it. Their very whiteness fills them with race guilt. They believe the triumph of the west was a triumph of white elitism and the subjugation and exploitation of non-white peoples. They ignore all the benefits it has brought to the world. They believe western culture was a great set-back for humanity, a mistake that should be corrected. So how does one go about destroying a civilization?

Stage one. Control the message. Indoctrinate the young. Teach them to reject the old values in favour of a new, opposing set of values. Turn history upside-down. Turn the nation's heroes into villains.

Stage two. Prepare the ground. Start a political protest movement. Make some noise. Get some publicity.

Stage three. Wait for the inciting incident.

Something bound to incite rage like the murder of George Floyd.

Stage four. Riot and social unrest. The gathering of committed followers willing to die for the cause.

Stage five. Insurrection. Revolution.

It begins with tearing down a nation's heroes, twisting its history, attacking its values and its cherished institutions. These are the pillars on which a civilization rests. Society needs heroes. Not celebrity heroes, or comic-book imitations. Real heroes, men and women of indomitable courage and rock-solid integrity. Heroes are the cement that holds a society together. They are the symbols of a nation's greatness. Without heroes to worship, a society can't feel itself to be great. It lacks self-confidence. It feels inferior. A nation without heroes is crippled and already half-defeated.

So where have all the heroes gone? They crept quietly down the back stairs in 1968, around the same time Martin Luther King Jr and Robert Kennedy were murdered. Anarchy and revolt were in the air. Young men had taken to the unspeakable practice of wearing flowers in their hair and burning the American flag in front of the White House. The Vietnam War was in full swing. Anti-war protests and race riots were tearing the country apart. American cities were going up in flames. It was a time not unlike our own.

People began to question the values America stood for. They lost faith in their leaders. Started to doubt their history and suspect the great deeds of the heroes they'd been taught to adore wasn't the truth. They were tired of the old stories. They longed for new heroes. So in a defiant act of lunacy they chose a handsome, romantic, revolutionary called Che Guevara and the mad, murderous dictator, Mao Tse Tung, as idols of worship. Che was a celebrity hero. Mao was the real deal, a genocidal hero who led his people into misery, destitution and slavery. That's the trouble with heroes. Their position is never entirely safe. Their deeds are always open to interpretation.

People grew ever more cynical as their leaders were revealed to be liars and crooks and the nation's capital exposed as a cesspit of corruption and criminality. America had somehow gone from the land of the free and the home of the brave to the land of the freebie and the home of the depraved. America's idols had feet of clay. The American dream was a hoax. It was all a fiction, a fairy tale for children. The heroes crept from the building because they were no longer wanted, no longer believed in.

Today's heroes are celebrity chefs, fashion designers, athletes, movie stars, talk show hosts, TV presenters and victims of injustice, sexual harassment and child abuse. One of our most outstanding heroes, Oprah Winfrey, the queen of the weepy eye, has turned self-pity into family entertainment. Oprah is the song-bird of sympathy, the siren of sorrows. No sob story is too maudlin, no trivial hurt beneath notice, no teardrop unrecorded. Oprah has made a vast fortune exploiting the misery market. There's big money to be made in Self-Pity City.

Funny, sitting here I can't think of another contemporary hero worth mentioning. Nelson Mandela comes to mind, but he's dead and his legacy of forgiveness is dying. I'm wracking my brains trying to come up with the name of a live hero and I'm coming up blank. I can't think of anyone but celebrity chefs, movie stars and stand-up comedians who fail to make me laugh. I'm perched on an empty pedestal and can't see a genuine hero anywhere. That's sad and a little frightening.

Hero-worship is the deep taproot that nourishes both religion and revolution, stability and chaos. Every church service is an act of hero-worship. So is every rock concert and political rally. Society is founded on hero-worship. Civilization is a hierarchy of ranks, of graduated hero-worship. When the ordinary citizen loses faith in his nation's heroes, when he discovers they're hollow and counterfeit, radical change is on the way, revolution is in the air.

Hero-worship has become deeply unfashionable. Yet, the urge to worship a hero is still there, as strong as ever. So, out of embarrassment, we give it different names. Worshippers of singers, actors and athletes are called fans. Worshippers of political leaders are called supporters. The worship of religious leaders is called veneration. We avoid the term hero-worship because it shames us and makes us feel small. Hero-worship suggests subservience, bowing down to a human being greater than ourselves. Such kow-towing is too oriental for western tastes.

The reputations of great men are always vulnerable. Critics love nothing more than cutting them down to size, their own small size. Take a Luther or a Lincoln. Critics explain that personal qualities such as courage, integrity and the determination to overcome insurmountable obstacles had nothing to do with their greatness. They were men and women of their time, thrown up by the emergencies of their time. The times made them inevitable. Time and circumstances did it all. No matter how much they whittle away, these small, nit-picking critics can't eradicate the secret reverence for heroes. It is buried too deeply in the human heart.

48

THE GENDER WARS

WHERE HAVE THEY gone, the gentle, submissive ladies of yesteryear? The dutiful, obedient wife? The loving stay-at-home mom? The contented house frau? The delicate creature waiting in the doorway with the bloom of contentment on her cheek? Did such women ever exist? Or did men just make them up?

The last fifty years have seen explosive changes in the way we live and the ideas we believe. One of these changes has been the empowerment of women. The long battle for female equality has been largely successful. Feminism, for the most part, has been a good idea, a righteous cry for justice and freedom. But like all good ideas it can be pushed too far and lead to a kind of despotism.

Even democracy itself can be pushed too far. Look what happened in England under Cromwell and in France under Robespierre. Tyranny and terror, heads rolling. Blood spatter before bedtime.

Today, women are wielding the axe. And heads are rolling. Everyday news stories report the fall of another powerful male, from CEO's to respected politicians, to Hollywood producers. The balance of power has shifted. The feminist mystique has triumphed. Women can claim victory. They've won the war. Yet the fighting in the erogenous combat zone is as fierce as ever. Why? Why does this senseless war drag on and on? Women have gotten the vote, the right to inherit property, to conduct their own financial affairs, to receive equal pay for equal work, to sue for divorce and scoop up most of the unwanted husband's assets. Men have been cowed. They stand with heads bowed like naughty schoolboys waiting to be spanked. What else can women want?

In order to keep this war of the sexes going a big lie is spreading like the Black Death through the western democracies. It is a lie that is intended to poison and divide and keep the fires of revolution burning bright and hot. "Things have never been worse!" cry these insurgent liars. "Misogyny, racism, homophobia, transphobia, islamophobia, xenophobia, anti-Semitism and white nationalism are again on the march. The hard-won battle for human rights is under threat. Democracy itself is in peril. To the barricades!"

This lie is huge, absurd and dangerous. A great many people have actually come to believe it, despite the overwhelming evidence to the contrary. In terms of human rights things have never been better in the west. Governments have never been more sympathetic, or sensitive to the needs and aspirations of minorities. Major corporations have all fallen into line for social justice, hiring people they never would have considered in the past, forcing employees to take diversity courses and behave appropriately around the water cooler. The mainstream media never misses an opportunity to parade their ultra-liberal credentials as advocates of civil liberties and human rights. They bend over backwards and drop their drawers if necessary to support strident minority demands. On the university campuses, in the social science departments, dreamy professors are relentlessly preaching utopian nonsense seeming unaware that every attempt to build a utopia has ended in a nightmare.

And yet the discontented minorities, with feminists leading the pack, tell us things have never been worse. That goose-stepping is back in fashion. That the swastika will soon be flying over the White House, and the British Parliament. If we dare to doubt this absurd lie we are punished, banded a racist, or a fascist, or a fool too stupid to understand what's happening. In the face of such fierce opposition sensible people keep their heads down and their mouths shut. That is exactly what happened in Nazi Germany. There is complicity in silence.

At the very bottom of feminist belief is the idea that women are morally superior to men. That they would do a much better job of running the world. Could this be true?

A case can be certainly made to support this notion. Women, not men, made civilization possible. They invented agriculture, the very foundation of human society. When the men were out hunting the hairy mastodon to extinction, women were planting seeds and growing crops. Women invented cookery, the beginning of science, making mastodon stew a tender and tasty treat. They invented family life, the very glue that holds society together. They tamed the Wild West. When the women moved in, the saloons and gambling halls closed down, churches and meeting houses sprang up in their place. They brought God along with law and order to town. Women not only invented civilization, they made it civilized. Without women to keep them in line men would be little more than savages. The one advantage men have over women is physical strength. This has always been the key to male domination. 'Do as I say or I'll kick the shit out of you.' In all other respects women have always proved to be the equal of men. Equal, not superior.

Women, too, have an advantage. Perhaps the decisive advantage. Sexual allure. So powerful is this attraction it causes level-headed men to lose their reason. They throw caution and common sense to the winds and turn themselves into panting dogs. But it doesn't stop there. Female tears have atomic power. They can melt the stoniest alpha-male heart. Women are master manipulators: the loving kiss, the whispered suggestion and men fall all over themselves to please these fragrant, insinuating creatures.

If women made civilization possible, men made it safer and more comfortable. Architecture was invented by men. (Probably to please a woman who wanted a roof over her head). Men invented all the labour-saving devices that freed women from the endless drudgery of household chores. The washing machine, the tumble drier, the vacuum cleaner, the automobile, the electric light, the TV set that babysits the kids, and a thousand other things – including lipstick and nylon stockings – that make the lives of women much more agreeable.

Now the very masculinity that protected women since the dawn of history is being called into question. Men, especially white men, have become anathema. Masculinity, itself, has become toxic. The male has been demoted from hero to a knuckle-dragging, dick-swinging, Neanderthal brute. Feminists insist that we become more feminine. "Off with their balls!" they cry. There seems to be a systematic campaign afoot to undermine male self-esteem. On television and in the movies men are portrayed as incompetent simpletons, nincompoops with learning difficulties. Or the very personification of evil, suggesting that every man is a Ted Bundy at heart. The object of this campaign is to socially castrate men, to strip them of their dignity and their manhood and reduce them to worker bees serving the queen.

These campaigners don't comprehend the damage they are doing, or its consequences. Take away a man's manhood, make him ashamed to be male, insult, dishonour, disgrace and humiliate him is a sure way to create an army of Ted Bundy's boiling with rage and a craving for revenge.

The feminists have powerful allies in their tireless efforts to stamp out masculine toxicity. Plenty of submissive men are on their side, happy to be led by the nose to the gelding shed. Then there are the gays and the lesbians and maybe the bisexuals, but the bisexuals are always equivocal. The only ones not to fall into line are the transgenders. The feminists strongly object to nutless geezers claiming to be real women. And with good reason. All a second-rate male athlete has to do to become a first-rate female athlete is to change his name from Donald to Daisy, put on pearls and pink panties and enter sporting events as a woman. He doesn't even have to have his nuts cut off. Size, bone structure and muscularity will make the difference. So an almighty row has broken out between these two groups. All is not sunshine and roses in the tangled camps of the militant minorities.

Male dominance was certainly one of the bad ideas that harmed the human race. It turned the institution of marriage from one of love and mutual respect into a master-slave relationship.

A dog, a wife and a walnut tree,

The more you beat them the better they be.

There is as much truth in that rhyme as there is in the feminist's slogan describing men: "Fifty per cent of America is one hundred per cent nasty." Clever, but empty, and untrue. I see no evidence that female dominance holds out the promise of a better world. All I see is the same old jackboot transferred to a female foot. In those times when women had the whip hand – I'm thinking of Margaret Thatcher, Golda Meier, Indira Gandhi, Elizabeth the 1st and so on. All of these women ruled with an iron fist as hard and as ruthless as any man's. They took no shit and little advice from their male colleagues and exerted all their power to the full. No delicate creature with the bloom of contentment on her cheek. More a cold, calculating Cardinal Richelieu playing deadly games of realpolitik.

The feminists seem intent on building a system of dogmatic beliefs embodied in a strong organization. The purpose is to influence opinion and politics and lead the gullible down the garden path to a golden future where justice and female supremacy reign unopposed. I have a strong suspicion that the garden path these pilgrims tread leads to a bitter stalemate between the sexes. Or the breakup of the movement.

History shows that when revolutionary movements achieve their goals they get greedy and push for more and more. They never know when to stop, to sit back and enjoy their victory. They have to go that one step too far, the fatal step that turns the tide against them. The feminists would do well to quit while they're ahead. But they won't. They love the fight too much. The movement gives them a sense of solidarity and companionship. It brings meaning and excitement to their lives. Without it life would be a grey, humdrum, lacklustre affair. Without it they would be lonely and, horror of horrors, might have to resort to the toxic male penis for a little entertainment.

It's just not enough that women should win. More importantly, men must lose.

49

THE DEPLORABLE
WHITENESS OF BEING

WHITE WORKING-CLASS PEOPLE aren't much liked by the cultural elite. Intellectuals look down on them with withering contempt. Politicians lie to them and speak to them as if they were backward children. The Politically Correct media constantly lectures them and keeps them distracted with fatuous reality shows that turn them into compliant voyeurs, easy to manipulate. At best they're patronized. At worst demonized. These elites are convinced that the ordinary citizen is a low, vulgar, moronic sub-human with bad table manners and violent tendencies. They wished such people didn't exist. But they grudgingly recognise their usefulness. The masses have two functions vital to the successful operation of a vibrant economy. Work and shopping. Civilization needs wage slaves and culture depends on consumers.

How did this animus begin? It seems to have started in the late 19th century with the introduction of the education act, which meant the lower orders were taught to read and write. Popular newspapers sprang up to feed this new hunger for the written word. Cheap, romantic novels began to appear and, even more alarming, people began to learn things they weren't supposed to know. Revolutionary ideas began to stir in the slums and the sweatshops. Those at the top began to worry.

Every democracy faces two connected problems. How to maintain social cohesion while, at the same time, granting its citizens freedom. Totalitarian regimes face no such problems. They arrest, torture and execute those who speak out in protest. Nothing terrifies the cloistered elites more than the people, the great seething majority that from time to time rises up in fury and overturns the established order. That's why our masters go to great lengths to keep us placid and quiet. That's why they hate us. That's why we're so deplorable. They hate what they fear. There are so damn many of us. When the rioting starts the smell of shit drifts down the mansions on the hill.

In 1930, a Spanish philosopher by the name of

José Ortega y Gasset published a small book called *The Revolt of the Masses*. This book summed up everything that was wrong with popular culture. José was pissed off with the masses. He hated the swarms of humanity crowding the cafés and the theatres, crawling like cockroaches over the beaches and the beauty spots, filling the parks and the public spaces, and polluting the overcrowded cities with their odious presence. Even worse, they were invading the sacred enclaves of the elite, pushing brazenly into places they didn't belong. Such impudence made José's blood boil. He saw this as a revolt.

He wasn't alone. In England, France, Germany and the United States the intellectuals were up in arms. Canonized writers like George Bernard Shaw, H.G. Wells, W.B. Yeats, D.H. Lawrence, E.M. Forster, Virginia Woolf and even the ultra-liberal pacifist, Aldous Huxley, advocated drastic measures such as eugenics and mass extermination to solve the problem. This solution was finally implemented in the gas chambers of Nazi Germany. Intellectuals can be monsters too.

Much of what Gasset wrote echoed an earlier German philosopher by the name of Fredrick Nietzsche. For a philosopher, Fred was unusual. He could actually write with verve and style in language people could understand. He was a master of the aphorism and the punchy one-liner.

All the above writers were huge Nietzsche fans. When he said: "Where the rabble drink, all the fountains are poisoned," they believed him. When he said: "Too many are born and they hang on the branches much too long," they believed him. When he prayed for "a storm to shake all this rottenness and worm-eatenness from the tree," they got down on their knees and prayed for the same thing. Eventually, they got what they prayed for: two world wars that significantly reduced the cockroach population.

The spectre that haunted their collective nightmares was hyper-democracy – the tyranny of the masses, where the individual would cease to exist. Democracy was anti-individualism. There would be no place for the lone voice of the literary genius. Art would be vulgarised and degenerate. Politics would cater to the mob. High culture would disappear to be replaced with mindless, feel-good drivel. Everything would flatten out in a multi-cultural soup that worshiped the average and despised the exceptional. This nightmare terrified the cultural elites. They must have woken up screaming.

After the Second World War the menace of Communism loomed large. The lumpen proletariat had become more frightening and despicable than ever. The Commie cockroaches had gobbled up more than half of Europe and were hungry for more. And, terrifyingly, they had the atomic bomb. These semi-literate sub-humans had the power to destroy life on earth. They were after nothing less than world domination. The terrified elites reached for the toilet paper.

Attitudes in the west began to change. Loathing for the 'basket of deplorables' was no longer fashionable, at least on the surface. The bewildered herd needed love and care to keep them mute and docile. The 1950's saw an explosion of consumerism. Shiny new home appliances flooded the market. Huge, baroque automobiles armoured with gleaming chrome could be bought on the instalment plan. Suburbs sprang up with neat little houses the working man could afford with a thirty-year mortgage. The economy was booming. Defence plants were churning out weapons of mass destruction. Families sat contentedly in the evenings eating TV dinners in front of their flickering black and white twelve-inch television screens watching *I Love Lucy*. Everything was wonderful.

Except it wasn't.

The political right was in the ascendant, busy dismantling the gains the labour movement had made during the reforming Roosevelt era. Government workers had to sign loyalty oaths. The mere suggestion of Communist sympathies meant unemployment. The Hollywood ten, who refused to rat on their friends, lost their careers and were led away in handcuffs to prison. Senator Joe McCarthy was tearing apart innocent people who testified before his subcommittee. Julius and Ethel Rosenberg were executed for passing atomic secrets to the Russians. A toxic atmosphere of paranoia and distrust hung over that time like a poison cloud. And that cloud has never gone away.

Things haven't changed much since the long ago 1950's. We in the west are still breathing in the same toxic atmosphere of paranoia, hostility and distrust. Communism may have collapsed along with the Berlin wall, but Marxist ideas are still alive and well, bubbling subversively in the ranks of the oppressed minorities. The ideology is the same, but the aims are different. Instead of a class struggle it's a race, gender, identity struggle. Just as in the 50's the poisoned cloud of paranoia, hostility and distrust is stifling public debate. People are afraid to speak out.

The category of deplorables has been whittled down to beer-swilling white men wearing baseball caps and smoking politically-incorrect cigarettes. These ignorant, dim-witted honkies hold racist, misogynistic, homophobic and xenophobic views. Even if they've never expressed such views, they certainly think them. White has become the new black. The tables have turned. The old prejudices have just switched colours.

Blacks fought for equality. So did women. So did the homosexuals. But at the point of victory something changed. Equality wasn't enough. It was decided that some were more equal than others. Since people of colour, women, homosexuals and transsexuals were the oppressed the moral high ground was theirs, and that made them more equal than the rest of us. This bad idea of superiority has been the source of much mischief as well as amusement. I can't help laughing every time I see white politicians humble themselves and offer grovelling apologies for the slave trade, an evil they had nothing to do with. I shake my head in despair when cowardly universities cancel the lectures of intimidating white men because some cowering co-ed might feel unsafe. I smile warmly every time a homosexual couple get hitched, convinced that with every such marriage a gay angel gets their wings. I seethe with indignation when a hulking male athlete is allowed to enter a women's sporting event. The world has gone mad. We've arrived at wit's end.

Reason itself is under threat. The whole idea of rationality as a moral and political justification has fallen into disrepute. The very thing that makes us human is being tossed overboard to make way for the lunacy of raw emotion. Reason, the minorities cry, is not interested in discovering the truth, but in protecting the power and the privilege of the one who reasons. Before we swallow this glib crap we should remember Goya's chilling remark: "The sleep of reason breeds monsters."

None of this would have been possible without the foolish connivance of the toxic white male. The white man has only himself to blame for his fall from grace. His bleeding heart, his empathy for the downtrodden and his race guilt over long-dead horrors has caused him to act against his own best interest, to side with the sinister forces of Political Correctness. His uneasy conscience has danced him into the dungeon of the deplorables where he'll remain for some time. Folly has a price.

I have a dream that I'll wake up one morning transformed into a black homosexual Muslim with transgender tendencies, that I'll be cleansed of my horrid whiteness and be welcomed with open arms into the ranks of the oppressed minorities that have become so aggressively oppressive. To date no miracle has taken place. Alas, I'm doomed.

50

WHY ARE THE OPPRESSED ALWAYS SO VIRTUOUS?

IN SEPTEMBER 1957 a shocking photograph appeared in newspapers around the world. It showed a Negro girl in Little Rock, Arkansas, being chased out of a white high school by a mob of white students shouting abuse. The face of one white girl stood out. It was filled with hate and horribly contorted with a malicious rage. By contrast the Negro girl was dignified and self-controlled. The picture shocked the world and shamed America. Even the bigots in the south were disturbed. The message was clear. The expression of the Negro girl symbolized good, and the face of the white girl symbolized everything that was evil and bad. I believe that was the moment when the colour white began to take on a darker hue.

The downtrodden of the world certainly deserve our sympathy, but the truth is they are just as rotten as the rest of us. Perhaps more so. Poverty, lack of education and opportunity doesn't promote virtue, or good behaviour. Rather the opposite. One of the many persistent lies that infect our age is the lie that some sections of the human race are morally superior to others. Both the mainstream media and the social media push this lie for all it's worth. They push it because supporting it makes them feel virtuous, and it makes the downtrodden objects of pity, needing their understanding and support.

So who are these pitiable creatures? In the west they can be easily identified. The poor, blacks, gays, Latinos, lesbians, bisexuals, women, the disabled and transgender people. According to the popular myth all of these groups are made up of gentle, generous, open-minded, intelligent, peace-loving individuals. These people would never break the law, get drunk, take illegal drugs, make racist remarks, insult their neighbours, beat their children, stab their significant others during a domestic, or do any of the nasty things that go in the white, middle-class suburbs.

The admiration for these disadvantaged groups allows no dissenting voice. Those foolish enough to ask awkward questions are quickly brought to book. They lose their jobs and their reputations. They become unemployable, marginalised, outcasts, disgraced and shunned for their heretical scepticism. They are shamed and brutally silenced, crushed under the merciless jack-boot of the social media.

There is a snarling beast stalking the land sniffing out heretics and free-thinkers to devour. This beast is the most dangerous beast of all. It is a bad idea with popular appeal. The world is no stranger to bad ideas. Nazism was such an idea. So was Stalinism. So was Maoism. This particular idea was hatched like so many bad ideas in the cloistered hothouse of academia. In this case Berkley, California. It was conceived with the best of intentions. To make the world a kinder, better place. Who could object to that? But, like all bad ideas, it wasn't properly thought through, the consequences never fully considered. Today, we are living with those consequences.

The name of this beast is Political Correctness, AKA Woke. Its purpose is to purge the world of all those horrid evils that make people unhappy. To rid the world of insult and nastiness. To ban hurt feelings. A noble aspiration, a utopian ideal quite impossible to achieve. The prophets of Political Correctness aren't stupid. They know a perfect world is beyond human reach, but that doesn't stop them from grasping for the golden ring of perfection. The closer they get the better the world will be. That's the theory. In practice things are very different. As I understand it Political Correctness is about language and the way we use it. As one definition states: *the avoidance of forms of expression or action that are perceived to exclude, marginalise, or insult groups of people who are socially disadvantaged or discriminated against.* On the face of it that sounds pretty reasonable. But there is a fly in the ointment. The word 'perceived'. Who is this anonymous perceiver? Is it a single individual, or a group? Maybe it's an outsider, not part of the group involved, simply a witness whose perception might be wrong, or biased.

This is the fly that poisons the ointment. Perception is a tricky thing. It isn't always right. It's a feeling and often depends on our mood, supported by our dislikes and prejudices. An innocent remark, an ill-judged joke, an inappropriate gesture or a silly tweet can be perceived as insulting, racist, or homophobic. The word 'perceived' is not forensically precise. It opens the door to all kinds of cruelty and injustice. It is a kangaroo court where the accused doesn't stand the ghost of a chance. Perception is a quicksand made for victims.

Open a newspaper on any given day and you're

likely to find a story about some hapless person who's wandered into the quicksand completely unaware that they are about to be swallowed up by the Media Monster, the ravenous offspring of Political Correctness. In the time it takes to smoke a politically-incorrect cigarette a life can be destroyed. A person who minutes earlier had a good job, a sterling reputation and the respect of their community suddenly finds himself, or herself, unemployed, unemployable, publically shamed, covered in Twitter shit, their reputation trashed, respect turned to scorn, shunned by their friends.

All it takes to accomplish the destruction of a life is just one person with a few hundred followers on Twitter to see something he, or she, *perceives* to be offensive. The perceived offensive remark is re-Tweeted and the chain-reaction begins. It races around the world at the speed of light inciting outrage, stirring up hatred and dreams of torture. By the time our hapless victim has finished the politically-incorrect cigarette, life as he or she knew it is over. The solid citizen has become a leper, a diseased, unclean creature spreading pestilence and pollution. A disgusting horror to be avoided for fear of contamination.

Does this seem right? How did a benign movement like Political Correctness morph into a vicious kangaroo court, a world-wide lynch mob? At some point, Political Correctness began to take on the characteristics of a new religion, a hard, puritan religion without God and without forgiveness. In the early stage new religions are always fierce and merciless when it comes to destroying its opponents and its heretics. This phase is always unpleasant if not downright evil. If it persists and is successful the result is an era of stagnation, a new dark age.

Lives aren't the only things being destroyed. Language itself is under attack. Perfectly good words are being stricken from the vocabulary. A few examples will suffice. 'Fat' is forbidden. 'Mankind' is offensive. 'Homosexual' is beyond the pale. 'Housewife' is abhorrent. 'Man-made' is even more abhorrent, and 'Sportsmanship' is insulting to female athletes. There are hundreds, perhaps thousands, of examples of the language being whittled down, shaped, and twisted to suit a political agenda. Language, written and spoken, is one of the glories of the human mind. It is the devise that allows us to think, to create, to communicate, to pass on what we've learned down the centuries. Language, along with mathematics, is what has lifted us from the cave to the penthouse, from struggling-to-survive-monkeys to the lords of creation. We have become god-like creatures with the ability to penetrate every mystery, except the mystery of our own existence.

Since language allows us to think it is essential to change the language if we are to think correctly. There is no better book on this subject than George Orwell's masterpiece, *1984*. George was a seer. He lived in Politically Correct times. A time when Jews were deemed to be parasites and slaughtered on an industrial scale. A time when Stalin's five-year plans resulted in the starvation of millions. A time when communism promised hope and delivered only misery. He knew where good intentions lead. He understood utopian dreams are nightmares in the offing. Read *1984*. It an antidote to the poisoned Pablum we are being fed by the Politically Correct puritans who casually destroy lives and language with the blasé cruelty of schoolboys pulling the wings off flies.

Political Correctness is a bad idea with popular appeal. It has all the credentials to attract the downtrodden and the dispossessed. More importantly, it appeals to the young, educated, privileged men and women who've never experienced a suggestion of racial or gender abuse. They jump on the bandwagon, eager to do something meaningful with their lives, like changing the world for the better. It appeals to the crusaders, the warriors willing to march, to face the opposition and demonstrate their commitment to the cause.

Such zeal has won tremendous victories in the past. The civil rights movement in the 1960's comes to mind. I was there. I saw it happen. I saw the United States became a better country. But Political Correctness isn't making things better. It's making things worse. This altruism seems to bring out what Jung called "our shadow side", the side that projects all our feelings of inferiority, self-loathing, guilt and hate onto the *perceived* enemy. It's a desire to join a righteous cause, to give life a higher meaning, to serve the powers of justice and fair play, even if it means the destruction of innocent lives along the way. It's telling people what they must think and what they must believe. It's a form of liberal totalitarianism, and its punishments for doubts are terrible. Political Correctness even has its own room 101.

I must admit that I've never been on Twitter. Never even been tempted to investigate Twitter. From what I hear I think I'd rather check in to the Bates Motel, or take tea in Ed Gein's front parlour. It sounds like a snake pit full of venom and hatred. A fiendish engine room manufacturing punishment and shame. Or maybe that's just my *perception*.

People don't take Political Correctness seriously enough. They snicker at its mention. They think it's silly. Yet they condone it in subtle ways they hardly realise. In Britain there is a well-known middle-aged male artist who likes to dress up as a little girl. Not just any little girl, but a 19th century little girl, like Alice in Wonderland, or Little

Bo Peep. A harmless perversion in private. But in public it becomes something else. This guy is an exhibitionist. He likes to appear on TV talk shows with a bow in his hair and a cute frilly skirt. This is a man who deliberately makes himself look foolish and expects not to be laughed out of town. He expects to be taken seriously and he is taken seriously. When Little Bo Peep tip-toes in front of the cameras nobody bats an eyelid. Nobody laughs. Not a titter. When a man deliberately makes himself ridiculous he should expect to be ridiculed. No such thing happens. The audience applauds. When Little Bo Peep speaks everyone listens. It's incredible! Was I the only man in Britain to find this wildly hilarious?

Nobody laughed because they knew what would happen if they did. They'd be immediately branded with a horrible name and find themselves chewed to pieces in the fiendish engine room of Twitter. One laugh and it would be game over. So they shut up and knuckled under. That's what Political Correctness does. It makes people afraid to laugh.

Political Correctness is sneaky. It's also unfair and hypocritical. While Little Bo Peep was wowing TV audiences in Britain with his cute little skirt and vapid remarks another, rather darker scenario, was being played out across the Atlantic in the United States. A teenage girl was dressing for her prom. The dress she chose to wear was a red Chinese number. Big mistake. An even bigger mistake was to post photos of herself on Twitter. By the time the dance was over this hapless teen had been ripped to pieces in the fiendish engine room, accused of an unforgivable crime: cultural appropriation. The poor kid was punished for wearing a Chinese dress. What a realm of contradictions is the strange, twisted world of Political Correctness. Little Bo Peep is applauded for gender appropriation, assuming the persona of an underaged member of the opposite sex, while a kid in Utah is viciously attacked for daring to wear the clothing of another culture.

Bad ideas have darkened the world many times before. The Carthaginians sacrificed children to their god, Molach, tossed their squalling infants into the flames because they believed such a practice would bring a good harvest. Humans are gullible. They can be made to believe anything. They can be persuaded to do the unthinkable if their faith is strong enough. So we must be very careful in our choice of beliefs. If we aren't careful we could find ourselves marching backwards into a new dark age of ignorance, superstition and terror, a place where books and babies are fed to the flames.

51

THE WONDERFUL WORLD OF WORK

WORK IS A dirty word to some. To others work is a source of pride, of achievement, of status. The sort of work we do is often how we define ourselves. Unemployment is more than the loss of a job. It is a loss of identity, a disgrace, something to be ashamed of.

For most of human history work has been a curse, a punishment for being born into this fallen world. Work was nothing but back-breaking drudgery to be avoided, or undertaken only out of dire necessity, or extreme compulsion. Then, with the fall of feudalism, something very peculiar happened. A strange transformation took place.

Instead of work being a curse it became something desirable. Having a job was an achievement to be proud of. A job was a must-have for every man who called himself a man.

In the good old days when slavery was in fashion people were forced to work under the master's lash. During feudalism the serfs were forced to work the baron's land or be cast out to starve. To them work was sweat, pain, tears and exhaustion that offered no reward in return for their labour. Aristocrats, too, hated work except when it applied to the peasants. They shivered at the thought of manual labour, thought it demeaning and beneath them. Aristocrats would rather die than pick up a shovel.

Under communism everyone had a job, but nobody worked because it was impossible to win promotion by hard graft and dedication to the job. Promotions were handed on the basis of seniority alone. It was also impossible to be fired no matter how lazy, or incompetent you were. This lack of a work ethic is one of the main reasons why the Soviet Union collapsed. That and central planning, which is always doomed to fail. Under capitalism the compulsion is more subtle. Nobody is forced to work. You're perfectly free to starve and live in a cardboard box. So most people are eager to sell themselves in return for a wage. Strangely, we in the prosperous west have come to believe work is a noble undertaking, a civic duty, something one does to support the family and the community at large.

Clearly, work means different things to different people. In the east, work is still a pretty grim affair. People throw themselves off the roofs of factories rather than endure the terrible conditions the workplace imposes. In the west, which is still dominated by the protestant ethic, work is revered as something holy. It has become a secular religion. The crazy idea that personal salvation can be achieved through hard work, education and cut-throat competition was conceived way back in the year 1517 when an angry German monk called Martin Luther nailed a list of complaints to a cathedral door. This dangerous act kicked off the Protestant Reformation, a movement that changed the world forever. Luther broke the Catholic Church's power in northern Europe and released something new into creation, a hungry genie called Capitalism. The Protestants came to see material success as a sign of God's favour. This gave them the green light to amass all the wealth they could get their mitts on. The more money they squeezed out of the system the bigger God's smile.

The world of work is divided into two camps mutually hostile to each other. The employers and the employees, the bosses and the bossed. The bosses know the less they pay their workers the more profit they will make. The workers know this too and formed trade unions to protect their wages and benefits. The two sides entered into negotiations. When these broke down there were strikes, lockouts, busted heads and sometimes fatalities on both sides.

After the Second World War a balance between labour and capital was reached. This led to a kind of Golden Age that lasted until 1973 when things began to fall apart. The Arabs raised the price of oil by 70% and at the same time cut back production in protest against US support for Israel in the Yom Kippur War. Economic stagnation set in. This coupled with rising prices created a crippling new economic disease called stagflation.

In the 1980's under the 'friendly fascism' of Regan and Thatcher the old mixed economy that had worked so well was scrapped and replaced by a harsher 'greed is good' Capitalism that all but destroyed the trade unions and left the workers shivering like lambs with the smell of the wolf in their nostrils. With globalization came unemployment, lost industries and decaying cities. This also hit the middle-class hard. After the crash of 2008, the rich got richer and the poor lost their homes and slept in doorways. The United States began to resemble a banana republic, a small, elite class of the super-rich sitting on top of a huge impoverished, powder-keg population burning with resentment and anger. This is the South American model. In these countries there is no middle-class to act as a buffer between the rich minority and the oppressed majority who have nothing to lose but their chains.

The purpose of a middle-class is to absorb the best people from the underclass, thus depriving the poor of able leaders and thinkers who would otherwise stir up unrest and revolution. That's why so many Latin-American countries have a long history of revolutions, coups, assassinations and frequent changes of government. They failed to develop a healthy middle-class. The American middle class is the reason the United States has enjoyed political stability for so long. And now the middle-class is disappearing like an endangered species, hunted down and killed by the poachers who sit on the boards of the big banks and the transnational corporations.

And they've got technology on their side. Soon, we'll have driverless vehicles to replace all the truckers and the cab drivers and the managers and office staff they support. Another huge segment of the labour force gone forever. It's ironic that just when Uncle Scrooge got employees to swallow the fiction that work is not only a duty, but also a virtue, robots came along and took away the work. The industries not easily automated were shipped overseas marooning their stranded workers on Poverty Island. In the past the new technology created enough new jobs to replace the old ones. That's no longer the case. The jobs lost to automation, globalization and to the pandemic will never come back. The vampires of big business love high unemployment. A surplus labour force allows them to bleed the surviving workers even further. Those still lucky enough to have jobs will be forced to take pay cuts, work longer hours and accept fewer benefits if they want to keep them.

The CEO's of the multinational corporations all suffer from the same self-serving delusion: that they are creating prosperity for everyone. 'That a rising tide lifts all boats'. These are the same folks who've already presided over two major financial crashes in this century alone. The dotcom bubble in 2000 and the housing bubble in 2008. These are the folks who thought it was a good idea to destroy the trade unions, ship their industries overseas, increase unemployment, accelerate urban decay and rig the political system to make them richer and even more powerful. These are the folks whose greed will eventually bring America and the west down. The consequences of their actions are not their concern. Growth is what they are after. Growth is what they worship.

These elite men and women don't hold themselves accountable for the misery they create. Managing their business is an end in itself, independent of what is being managed. Expertise, not ethics, determines the agenda. The cost to the country and its people is simply collateral damage.

According to The Peter Principal every employee in a hierarchy rises to their level of incompetence. Or, to put it another way, those at the top probably shouldn't be there. Today, that is certainly the case. From dismal, sleepy Joe Biden, to the republican reptiles, to the disgraceful democrats, to the bloated billionaires and to the whole rotten ideology they represent.

Starve the poor. Feed the rich.

And screw every other son-of-a-bitch.

It's that kind of thinking that caused the French Revolution and the Russian Revolution and all those revolutions south of the border down Mexico way.

How can a smart, well-educated, civilized ruling class be so stupid, so incompetent, so greedy, and so blind not to see that if they continue to dismantle the safeguards that protect working people from destitution, then sooner or later the roof is going to cave in? Revolution will sweep the land. The statue of liberty will fall and the United States will become the new Venezuela.

To most Americans that's unthinkable. "No! No!" they cry. "Not America!" Why not America? Empires, like people, wither and die. Greece, Rome, Spain and Britain had their day in the sun. All of them lasted a long time. The United States by comparison has been the big dog for a mere 75 years and already the classic signs of decay are beginning to show. A remote ruling class completely out of touch with the mass of the people. Tremendous economic and racial inequality. Military failures. The reliance on propaganda to prop up a failing system. Social unrest at home and the collapse of courage on the part of local authorities too afraid to stop the looting and destruction of private and public property. America is sick and getting sicker.

The covid pandemic is radically changing the way work is organized. Millions of office workers were told to work from home. Others were paid to stay home and do nothing but watch daytime TV. Predictably, when the office workers were called back to the office, they didn't want to go back. They preferred to sit around in their pyjamas and work from home. Cosy for them, but a disaster for the people who depend on the office workers to eat in their restaurants and shop in their stores. If this is the future of work, city centres will become empty and deserted. The great office buildings will become shelters for the homeless and the surrounding streets will be dangerous with predators.

The Peter Principal demonstrates the reason why the west is in decline. Its leaders have all risen to their level of incompetence. They ain't up to the job and they are fucking things up for the rest of us. Nemeses is peeking through the window. Change is coming. The sun is gradually going down on the American dream.

52

How Much Freedom is Enough?

FREEDOM FALLS ROUGHLY into five main categories. Nation freedom, group freedom, intellectual freedom, economic freedom and personal freedom. To the majority of us personal freedom is the most important. Why should we obey anyone else? Why we are not allowed to do as we choose? And if we disobey, will we be punished? By whom and to what degree? In the name of what authority? For the sake of what law?

We in the west believe we are the freest people on earth, and we are compared with North Korea and Putin's Russia. But just how free are we? There's plenty of things we aren't allowed to do. If we break the law we lose our freedom. If we slack at work we lose our jobs. If we drink and drive we lose our licences. If we commit murder we lose our lives. So our personal freedom is limited, and rightly so. If everyone was allowed to do as they please whirl would be king. Anarchy would rule. Civilization as we know it would collapse along with our freedoms and civil liberties.

Total freedom is impossible. It is limited by governments, by the law, by economic circumstances, by social pressure and by cultural taboos. We must work whether we like it or not. We must fit in with our peers, even if the fit doesn't feel comfortable or right. We must be careful how we speak. Say the wrong thing and the sinister forces of Political Correctness will gather against you.

If you're a teacher, you won't be allowed to teach. If you're a politician you won't get re-elected. If you're a TV personality you'll disappear from the screen. If you're a journalist no publisher will print what you write. If you're an ordinary working person with no power or influence you have hardly any freedom at all. Violate a cultural taboo and you're free to eat out of a garbage can and make your home in a storm drain. It may be iniquitous, but some people have a lot more freedom than others. Democracy is never fair, and freedom favours those with wealth and status. The problem of personal freedom is one of degree.

Freedom for the ordinary Joe worried about his job, struggling to pay the rent, is a bright, shimmering mirage always out of reach. Only those with an independent income are free from slavery.

One way an individual can gain influence is by joining a group. In today's world very few individuals can have much influence unless they are a member of some organization. With the rise of sophisticated minority groups like people of colour, feminists, homosexuals and the transgender community, all clamouring for one freedom or another, all playing the oppressed minority card, democratic governments seem to be at a loss how to deal with them. Politicians, with the word 'freedom' continually in their mouths, can hardly criticize black people for demanding justice, to be free from persecution. Nor can they denounce women for demanding equality, or homosexuals for protesting against discrimination, or transgender men claiming to be females. Even when these groups go too far, when they demand the impossible, even when their activities reduce the freedom of others, the politicians contrive to look the other way, too afraid to speak out.

And they are not alone in their pusillanimous pandering. Broadcasters, celebrities, business leaders, anybody with a lot to lose shut their traps and gaze off into the distance. No one has the guts to ask one simple question: Should tolerance be granted to those groups that demonstrate *intolerance*, which systematically sets out to destroy the lives of those who disagree with them? Like Pontius Pilate they wash their hands and refuse to answer.

All minority groups, all oppressed people, believe they are fighting for human freedom. This provides an ideal to aspire to, adds a moral dimension to the longing for justice rooted in every persecuted individual. Victory, however, brings an abrupt volte face. Freedom won, the new privileges must be defended. In order to defend them, the freedom fighters take up the very weapons used against them and, ironically, become the new enemies of freedom. Many Latin-American countries lean towards this model. So do victorious minorities.

Under a repressive government intellectual freedom is the first to go. In the 19th century under a mildly repressive regime, Russia produced Dostoevsky and Tolstoy. These two men were engaged in subversive activities at one time or another. Dostoevsky was sent to Siberia, but was later reprieved when he wrote an ode dedicated to the empress. Tolstoy was too big a name to touch. Under benign repression, Russia was supreme in literature. Under Stalin things were very different. Writers who criticised the regime were ruthlessly liquidated, or sent to die in the gulags. Under

Stalin, Russian literature dwindled down to nothing of worth. Apart from the production of great works, freedom encourages self-respect and helps people to stand upright and do what their conscience dictates. In the 21st century such freedom is an endangered species.

We in the west believe we have freedom of thought. We're kidding ourselves. The news and entertainment media are owned by oligarchs who feed us Pablum and propaganda. They decide what we should think, the opinions we should hold. Democracy demands conformity. The social media is a new kind of beast, a hungry beast fond of demonising dissenters. Literature and free speech are under attack once again. A man writing fiction in the voice of a woman, or someone of a different race, is condemned and shamed for such a violation of identity. Imagination is taboo. Say something mildly unflattering to anyone of an oppressed minority and you're slapped in jail, accused of a hate crime. Your life is ruined.

There seems to be an innate impulse towards conformity in the human character. A herd instinct. No one wants to be out of step, or at odds with their fellows. To get along you go along. Those who don't go along are punished in all sorts of ways. Social ostracizing, unemployment and shame, to name but three. These days one must be economical when it comes to free speech.

Surveillance cameras are everywhere. So are video cameras. We are followed, tracked, photographed and watched 24/7. You can't take a shit without someone measuring the size of the turd. This may be good for law enforcement, but it does little for personal privacy. None of this sounds much like freedom to me.

Freedom can also be a burden too heavy to bear. It can be frightening, a threat, something to escape from. How many of us would like the load of decision and responsibility taken off our backs? Wouldn't it be wonderful to have a strong leader to carry it for us? Someone we can follow and believe in, someone who will clear up all the confusion, give us answers and tell us what to do. America looks to their president. Britain to the prime minister, Muslins to their ayatollah. Jews to their rabbi. In the hungry thirties, in the depths of the great depression, Germany looked to a man wearing a small moustache.

It is a mistake to suppose Hitler came to power through cunning and deception. He was democratically elected to power because the majority wanted a saviour. They were sick of freedom. Freedom took away their jobs. Freedom made their money worthless. Freedom gave them nothing but hopelessness and empty bellies. Hitler promised to fix all this on the condition that the Germany people give up this silly, abstract idea of liberty. Freedom died in Germany with hardly a whimper.

Freedom is a very fragile thing. It depends on a great many factors. Tolerance, economic stability and the crucial judgement of just how much freedom to allow. Where to draw the line between too much and too little. Too much and you have a tyranny of the majority. Too little and you have a troublesome underclass of malcontents and misfits stirring up social unrest. When things are going seriously wrong, mistakes must never be admitted. The media continue to pump out the Pablum and the propaganda. Happy, positive messages fill the airways. Or, if necessary, fear is used to remind us of how happy we are to be living in a democratic society. The external threat of terrorism or war is employed to restore conformity and take away some of our freedoms and protections. Surveillance is justified, suspension of habeas corpus is passed with little opposition, extraordinary rendition, in other words kidnapping becomes ok. So does illegal imprisonment and torture. Governments, even democratic governments, are always suspicious of freedom. The ordinary citizen shouldn't be troubled with weighty matters beyond their understanding. Pablum and propaganda are what they need and plenty of it.

We, the people, are seldom told the complete truth. We, the people, are more often lied to, palmed off with platitudes and catchy slogans that mean absolutely nothing. Knowledge *is* freedom. Without it freedom is a blind cripple stumbling around in an empty room. We in the west take our limited freedoms too much for granted. Freedom is always under threat and has many enemies. Ignorance, intolerance, propaganda, apathy, fear of the other, terrorism and zealous elected officials with their hands on the levers of power.

Freedom is an illusion, manufactured in Hollywood and on our TV screens. We aren't free. We are controlled, manipulated and hoodwinked, told what to think and how to behave. What's acceptable and what's not. We are free to move around, to change jobs, to get married to the person we love, and divorce the person we hate. We have many freedoms other societies don't enjoy, but some of them are gradually being whittled down, one by one, until the light of freedom is eventually extinguished.

53

ARE THE OLD REALLY HUMAN?

THERE IS NO shock more terrible than the shock of old age. It strikes with a bite that never lets go. Old age is nature's curse, the biological punishment for living too long.

But the punishment isn't merely biological. The old are outcasts, a disenfranchised group pushed to the margins of society. The world's parliaments, congresses and senates, places where the laws are made, tend to view the old as a burden, a drain on the resources of the state. No doubt politicians wish all these needy, useless pensioners would pull the plug, get it over with and die. The only time governments take notice of the old is at election time when they dangle empty promises to encourage the hobbling army of the decrepit to get out and vote.

Young people don't like the old much either. Aged faces and palsied limbs invoke impatience and irritation. The old are wrinkled, shrivelled and ugly. Hardly human. They creep, they drool. They mumble boring tales of the long-dead past no one wants to hear. They can't keep up. They can't work. They contribute nothing. They consume, but don't produce. What good are they?

That is a question the old often ask themselves. What good am I? Alas, for many there is no answer. All they know is what they are supposed to be, what society wants them to be. Silent and unseen, tucked away in their lonely rooms gathering dust in absolute serenity. If an old person should exhibit passion, jealousy, or sexual desire he or she is looked upon with loathing and disgust. The old are not supposed to feel such things. They are required to be virtuous, wise and above all, placid. Society likes to believe the old have sailed into a calm harbour beyond all fleshly concerns. If they should fall below the expected standard of virtue they become ludicrous, a disgrace, a laughing stock for children and an embarrassment to their relatives. It matters little if the old person chooses virtue or vice. Either way he or she is a creature of no importance, a waste product, an outcast. Society has no scruple in denying the old the support necessary to live like human beings.

Young adults live as if they will never grow old. Old age is unthinkable. It can't happen, not to me, they cry. It's too far in the future to worry about, so remote in time it merges with eternity, making it unreal. The young can't imagine that the strong, swift, healthy body they occupy is in the grip of a slow, destructive metamorphosis that will whiten their hair, pull their teeth, slow their walk, unsettle their balance, impair their hearing, dim their sight, fragment their memory, dull their mind, destroy their beauty and confine them to that lonely room to moulder in dusty serenity.

The young fail to understand that the treatment dished out to the old today will be allotted to them tomorrow. A story by Grimm cleverly illustrates this truth. A middle-aged peasant has banished his annoying old father from the dinner table, away from the rest of the family. The old man is forced to eat like a farmyard animal from a trough. One day the peasant finds his own son nailing some boards together. He asks the boy what he is doing. The boy tells him he is building a trough. "It's for you," the child says. "When you are old." The grandfather is immediately given back his place at the family table. If only things worked out so well in real life.

Nomadic societies are forced by necessity to

kill the old, or leave them behind to starve and die. These nomadic people have no room for the lame and the infirm. Yet they are kinder than some of the western democracies who have no room for the unproductive. The old aren't killed, or left to die, at least not yet. Instead, they are ignored, deprived of their humanity and stripped of their dignity. They are dependants of the state and treated like poor relations, with cruel indifference. The words 'old' and 'poor' couple tunefully together like love and marriage, like a horse and carriage.

Things are very different for the rich. Money provides care, comfort and security. The rate of physical decline depends on which class you belong to. For the rich and privileged decline is much slower than it is for the poor. A manual labourer is finished at sixty. The pampered banker can still be vigorously swindling the public at eighty. The poor are condemned to near destitution, slum housing, isolation, and a profound loneliness that results in a torpid bewilderment and a gloomy apathy that undermines an already fragile physical and mental stability. Money makes a huge difference, but it doesn't help a failing body. The rich and the poor share a common fate. Plutocrat or pauper, once the fire of life has flickered out and the zeal for living has died the ashes look about the same. When the memory decays and life begins to unravel, stitch by stitch, like a piece of frayed knitting, all the money in the world won't save you. Old age is nothing if not democratic.

Of all the animals, humans age the worst. Animals grow thin and feeble, but their outward appearance doesn't change that much. Humans, on the other hand, change beyond all recognition. The alteration is startling and total. The lovely young woman becomes an ugly crone with a crooked back and loose dentures. The handsome, youthful Galahad a shuffling ruin with a swollen prostate, high blood-pressure and bladder problems. Their looks are utterly transformed. They are unrecognisable, even to themselves. My heart is wounded every time I see a once beautiful movie star that I was half in love with humbled and ravaged by time.

We in the west are obsessed by youth and beauty. The word 'old' has all but been abolished. Nobody gets old anymore. They mature, they ripen, but they never, ever, become hoary. Terms such as crone, curmudgeon, geezer, venerable or any version of golden is forbidden. In fact, age isn't mentioned at all. Americans, in particular, are sensitive to labels such as senior citizen, elderly, pensioner, long in the tooth, washed-up, over the hill, old-timer, fogey and any other word or phrase that reminds them they are no longer young.

The old would do anything to regain their lost youth. They'd happily sell their soul to the devil, or drain the blood of a virgin if that would do the trick. Since the first isn't possible and the second is illegal they resort to less dramatic stratagems. Cosmetic surgery is at the top of the list, followed by fad diets and exotic therapies like bathing in baby urine. They emerge from the operating room with a weird, mask-like look, a cartoon caricature of themselves that fools no one. The fad diets leave them looking stringy and malnourished. The urine baths fill the air with a strong aroma of piss, but don't do a thing for the sags and wrinkles. None of it works. Once the sweet bird of youth has flown it will never return.

The hunt for the Fountain of Youth has moved on a bit since Ponce de Leon combed the jungles of Florida in a vain attempt to find it. The search has now retired to the laboratory where science is busy delving into the mystery of aging. Quite possibly science might find a way of slowing the process down and prolonging life to a remarkable age. Is this really a good thing? It would certainly cause a great social upheaval. Children would begin murdering their parents, impatient with having to wait another hundred years for their inheritance. Such a delay of death would rock civilization to its foundations. Personally, I don't think Mother Nature will take this meddling lying down. She will strike back, as she did with the superbugs that defy antibiotics. She will invent fiendish new diseases to confound the medical profession and torture the beneficiaries of this extended life-span.

What ever happened to the idea of growing old gracefully? It faded away with the death of God. Now we are the gods ruling over creation, yet we remain as mortal as ever, subject to the immutable laws that govern the universe. We rebel against this notion. Look how far we've come. We've made it all the way from the cave to the moon with nothing but our brains and our ingenuity to help us. We've explored the solar system, mapped the planets and sent probes into deep space. We've done God-like things. Why should we be chained to these slowly disintegrating bodies? Yet we are chained. And likely to remain so.

When the old can no longer look after themselves they face the final humiliation – the dreaded trip to the nursing home. For the rich this can be quite a pleasant experience offering professional care, private rooms, comfortable surroundings, beauty parlours, gymnasiums, physiotherapists, good food, organised activities and maybe a happy hour where everyone gets together for a friendly drink.

The poor can expect a very different set of circumstances. They are likely to end up in a seedy, substandard facility staffed by poorly-trained care workers on a minimum wage. A high percentage of these people will be young, dangerously stupid and unsympathetic to the plight of their patients. They will be slow to respond. They will feed you roughly, shoving the cheap, tasteless food down your throat as quickly as possible to get the whole disgusting business over with. They will forget to wipe your ass. They will smoulder with resentment at having to change soiled sheets and mop up the mess of those unfortunate little accidents caused by incontinence. Now and then the resentment will boil up into a rage and some helpless old fart will be throttled and punched for wetting the bed once too often.

Assault is not the only hazard the inmate of a nursing home must face. There is also the risk of fire. According to the Nation Fire Prevention Association, the most dangerous place to be in respect to fire is in a nursing home. The halt and the bedridden have little chance to escape the flames. In the event of fire the minimum wage care workers will sensibly save themselves, leaving the old to burn.

Don't think for a minute that these shabby, frightening firetraps, and all the thoughtless abuse and neglect they provide comes for free. It doesn't.

Nursing homes aren't charitable organizations. They exist to make a profit. Their first priority is the bottom line. At the moment, in Britain, the old person who has slaved and scraped to buy a house is forced to sell that house to pay for the dubious care he receives in the gloomy chambers of the nursing home. Only when all the money is gone will the government grudgingly step in to help the old who have been paying taxes all their working lives. It's a great scandal. Government after government has promised to look into it, but nothing is ever done.

Are the old really human? They are, but they aren't treated as such. At best they are looked upon as a nuisance. At worst, creatures belonging to a different species, placed somewhere between an ape and a dribbling idiot. Their reward for a lifetime of service is a miserable pension barely enough to live on. The old are victims of a system that has no use for the useless. The old are the outcasts of a throwaway society. They are nothing but rejects, cast-offs, broken down, worn-out pieces of machinery tossed on the scrapheap.

What can the old do about this festering injustice? Very little. They have no power, no influence, no inspiring leader to take up their cause. They have no voice. They are alone and helpless, at the mercy of forces over which they have no control. The old are in a pitiful situation, feeble, needy, dependent on others for help. They beg with their eyes. They must rely on kindness to survive.

The old might be powerless, but they do have a choice. A Shakespearian choice. To be or not to be. They can wait stoically, enduring the boredom, suffering all the indignities and pain that come with crumbling bodies. They can dream about the past and try not to think about the grim future that waits for them just around the corner. 'To be' invites anguish. 'Not to be' embraces peace.

When the black, gothic door of the nursing home looms open before me and the threatening hand of the care-worker beckons, I know what my choice will be.

The End

ABOUT THE AUTHOR

M.B. Walsh was born in Canada and educated at the University of Toronto. He is the author of five novels and an award-winning collection of short stories. He currently resides in the U.K.